The Pioneer Woman Cooks

DINNER'S READY!

The Pioneer Woman Cooks

DINNER'S READY!

112 FAST AND FABULOUS RECIPES
FOR SLIGHTLY IMPATIENT HOME COOKS

REE DRUMMOND

WM
WILLIAM MORROW
An Imprint of HarperCollinsPublishers

ALSO BY REE DRUMMOND

The Pioneer Woman Cooks: Super Easy!

The Pioneer Woman Cooks: The New Frontier

The Pioneer Woman Cooks: Come and Get It!

The Pioneer Woman Cooks: Dinnertime

The Pioneer Woman Cooks: A Year of Holidays

The Pioneer Woman Cooks: Food from My Frontier

The Pioneer Woman Cooks: Recipes from an Accidental Country Girl

Frontier Follies

The Pioneer Woman: Black Heels to Tractor Wheels

Children's Series

Charlie the Ranch Dog

Little Ree

HarperCollins books may be purchased for educational, business, or sales promotional use. For information, please email the Special Markets Department at SPsales@harpercollins.com.

FIRST EDITION

Designed by Kris Tobiassen of Matchbook Digital

Food photography by Ed Anderson

Lifestyle photography by Ree Drummond except the following: pages ii, viii, 64, 158, and 364 by Ashley Alexander; page 22 courtesy of the Abeyta family

Library of Congress Cataloging-in-Publication Data

Names: Drummond, Ree, author.
Title: The Pioneer Woman cooks: dinner's ready : 112 fast and fabulous recipes for slightly impatient home cooks / Ree Drummond.
Other titles: Pioneer woman (Television program)
Description: First edition. | New York : William Morrow, [2023] | Includes index. |
    Identifiers: LCCN 2023022328 | ISBN 9780062962843 (hardcover) | ISBN 9780062962874 (ebook)
Subjects: LCSH: Dinners and dining. | Quick and easy cooking. | LCGFT: Cookbooks.
Classification: LCC TX737 .D78 2023 | DDC 641.5/4—dc23/eng/20230515
LC record available at https://lccn.loc.gov/2023022328

ISBN 978-0-06-296284-3

23 24 25 26 27 LBC 5 4 3 2 1

To my family.

You're all my favorite.

Contents

Introduction

I'm Ree Drummond, and I'm an impatient home cook. Raise your hand if you're with me! (I hope you're raising your hand.)

Okay, don't get me wrong. I still love cooking. But over the past two or three years, so much in my world has changed. As of this year, all the kids are officially out of the house. When Ladd and I dropped off Todd at the University of South Dakota and hugged him goodbye, two things happened: First, I cried for three weeks straight.

Second, Ladd and I officially became empty nesters! So what was once a household of seven has finally been whittled down to two. In the months since Todd left, Ladd and I have been gradually adjusting to schedules that don't center entirely around teenagers and all their craziness: soccer, volleyball, football, curfews, supervising, grounding, blood, sweat, and tears. We both love it and hate it. The house is so quiet! It's terrible and it's wonderful. Empty nesting is not for the faint of heart.

Not to mention, I'm getting older, friends! And I'm hitting that stage wherein I'm being much more selective about what I spend my time doing. Some days I find myself having neither the focus nor the inclination to make long, drawn-out recipes for dinner. Not that Ladd and I alone aren't worth the effort—ha ha! (We are! I think.) It's just that I've gotten impatient! Selective! Over it? (Did I say that out loud?) And while I still want to cook something delicious for supper, I want to get in and out faster so I can go be the keeper of my own schedule, time, crossword puzzles, walks with the dogs, and reality TV marathons. Again, raise your hand if you're with me!

This cookbook (which might be my favorite to date!) was born out of this new cooking landscape in which I find myself. I've assembled a truly luscious lineup of fun food, flavorful food, and fantastically fabulous-tasting food . . . but food that's more doable than ever, and that takes less time and fuss than ever. And lest you think that means these recipes phone it in, nothing could be further from the truth! The only person who'll know how easy and simple these recipes are to cook is you.

And you, as the person doing the cooking, are what matters!

I hope you enjoy every single recipe, and the new family photos I share along the way. (The kids still come home to visit! And eat.) I hope you give yourself permission to take it easy in the kitchen, to use shortcuts, employ time-saving tricks, and grab store-bought substitutes if the mood strikes. I think you'll come away from this book with a bunch of new family favorites, and I hope you'll be inspired to get in the kitchen more, to get out of the kitchen more quickly (ha!), and to breathe in and enjoy life.

Lots of love,

Ree

XOXOXO

Flavorful Fridge Grabs

As a slightly impatient home cook, I'm a big believer these days in recipes that don't take forever to make. However, it's also very important to me that the food I serve to my friends and family tastes absolutely incredible. To that end, I have found that if I take some time every two or three weeks to whip up jars of the following dressings, relishes, and other accoutrements, the flavor payoff is totally through the roof. All these delights add a little extra something to your everyday recipes and can take something from delicious to utterly unforgettable without adding any more time to the recipe itself.

From slow-cooked garlic cloves to tangy pickled relish, I promise you will "grab" these little jars of heaven over and over again! They are gifts that keep on giving.

These little garlic cloves make Spinach Artichoke Pizza (page 216) sing!

GARLIC CONFIT

⏱ 5 MINUTES (PLUS 1 HOUR 45 MINUTES IN THE OVEN)   **MAKES ABOUT 1½ CUPS**

There's nothing better than roasted garlic . . . unless it's garlic confit! While garlic is usually roasted by drizzling with a little oil and baking until the cloves are soft and buttery, garlic confit is completely submerged in oil as it cooks in the oven, and I can't say enough about the absolutely miraculous flavor that ensues. Not only do you wind up with a jar full of nutty, luscious garlic to add to everything from mashed potatoes to pizza, you also get the flavorful oil that comes with it! You can drizzle it over fresh tomatoes, cooked pasta, or anything that needs a big infusion of garlic deliciousness.

Making garlic confit couldn't be easier, especially since you can now buy nice-size bags of peeled cloves. Yet another reason I'm glad I'm living in the new millennium! (*Real Housewives* is also on that list, btw. . . .)

1 generous cup peeled garlic cloves

2 rosemary sprigs

1 teaspoon red pepper flakes

Pinch of kosher salt

Olive oil, to cover (about 1 cup)

1. Preheat the oven to 275°F.

2. In a small baking dish, combine the garlic cloves, rosemary, pepper flakes, and the salt.

3. Add enough oil to cover the cloves.

4. Press down with a spoon to make sure the garlic and rosemary are submerged.

5. Cover the dish with foil . . .

6. And bake until the garlic is golden brown and very soft, about 1 hour 45 minutes.

7. Once the mixture is cooled, spoon the cloves into one 8-ounce or two 4-ounce jars, covering with the oil from the dish. Store in the refrigerator for up to 1 week, grabbing cloves as you need!

(Important: Do not store at room temperature.)

〰〰〰〰〰〰〰〰

WHAT TO DO WITH IT

- *Add several cloves (to taste!) to a batch of mashed potatoes.*
- *Stir into macaroni and cheese.*
- *Spread on bread as the base of panini.*
- *Use to top baked pizza.*
- *Include a little dish of it as part of a charcuterie board.*
- *Keep the vampires away!*

PICKLED PEPPERS

🕐 12 MINUTES (PLUS 1 HOUR TO PICKLE) **MAKES ONE 16-OUNCE JAR**

You know what? It's terrible to be well into middle age and suddenly discover that one of your favorite tongue twisters of all time has completely misled you. I just now realized that Peter Piper could not actually have picked a peck of pickled peppers. After all, peppers don't grow out of the ground already pickled. One must pick the peppers, then pickle the peppers, and it is quite impossible to pick peppers that have already been pickled, because one has to pick them before pickling them.

I'm exhausted now. But oh, these pickled peppers! They will add some zing to your food and some spring to your step. I adore them!

6 to 8 chile peppers (jalapeño, Fresno, mini sweet)

⅔ cup rice vinegar

2 tablespoons honey

½ teaspoon mustard seeds

½ teaspoon red pepper flakes

½ teaspoon kosher salt

3. Bring the mixture to a boil and turn off the heat.

6. Let the contents cool to room temperature, then screw on the lid.

1. Thinly slice the peppers and discard the stems. Remove more seeds from the hotter peppers if you like less spice!

4. Layer the peppers in a 16-ounce mason jar, packing them tight as you go.

7. Turn the jar upside down a couple of times to mix. Store the peppers in the fridge for 24 hours before eating. They'll keep in the fridge for 1 month.

WHAT TO DO WITH THEM

- *Add a few to the top of burgers.*
- *Sprinkle them over pizza.*
- *Add them to a roast beef sandwich.*
- *Decorate the top of nachos.*
- *Serve as a garnish for tacos.*
- *Place inside a grilled cheese sandwich!*

2. In a small saucepan, combine the vinegar, honey, mustard seeds, pepper flakes, salt, and ⅔ cup water.

5. Carefully pour the hot liquid over the peppers, pushing down the peppers as needed with a spoon until they're submerged.

Peter Piper would love these peppers on this Chicken Apple Sage Burger (page 241)!

PEPPERY RANCH DRESSING

🕐 *12 MINUTES* **MAKES 2 CUPS**

What can we say about ranch that hasn't already been said? It's the official condiment of the state of Oklahoma (not really, but it should be) and in its most basic form, it's a downright perfect concoction that goes with absolutely everything. For goodness' sake, I have a son who dips individual bites of medium-rare ribeye steak in ranch. I have another son who pours ranch over his pizza. I have a daughter who conditions her hair with it! Just kidding on that last part, but what I'm saying is that ranch has officially taken over the world.

It's hard to improve on the original, but I think "peppering" (pun intended) ranch with ground pepper actually does make it more delicious. It adds a little extra heat and flavor, and the result is something utterly memorable!

1 cup mayonnaise

½ cup sour cream

1 garlic clove, peeled

¼ cup fresh flat-leaf parsley leaves, minced

2 tablespoons minced fresh dill

1 tablespoon minced fresh chives

1 tablespoon tricolor peppercorns, crushed

½ teaspoon ground black pepper

1 teaspoon Worcestershire sauce

Dash of hot sauce

Pinch of kosher salt

¼ to ½ cup buttermilk (as needed for the desired consistency)

1. In a medium bowl, combine the mayonnaise and sour cream.

3. Sprinkle in the herbs . . .

5. Add the Worcestershire, hot sauce, and salt . . .

2. Press or finely mince the garlic and add it to the bowl.

4. And the crushed peppercorns and the ground black pepper.

6. Then add ¼ cup of the buttermilk . . .

A Surprise Burger (page 233) with this peppery ranch dressing is an inspired combo!

7. And stir until everything is combined. Add the remaining ¼ cup buttermilk if you like a slightly thinner consistency. Taste and adjust the seasonings (the garlic flavor will deepen as it sits in the fridge!).

8. Transfer the dressing to a mason jar and keep in the fridge for up to 10 days.

~~~~~~~~~~~~~~~~~~~~~

WHAT TO DO WITH IT

- *Serve on an iceberg wedge (or any salad!).*
- *Use as a dip for carrots and celery.*
- *Serve with Buffalo wings.*
- *Use as a dipping sauce for chicken nuggets, fries, or pizza!*

His smile still weakens my knees.

ZIPPY VINAIGRETTE

⏱ 5 MINUTES **MAKES 2 CUPS**

There are millions of vinaigrette recipes out there. Billions, even! And most of them are pretty fine. Delicious, even! So I've had to tweak and adapt mine through the years to keep my tastebuds from having a midlife crisis like the rest of my person is doing. I won't go into detail. I can hear you thanking me.

Anyway, where I've finally landed in my vinaigrette journey is this very citrus-forward dressing that's just perfect for anything that needs a slightly sweet, very tangy, and exceedingly herbaceous kick!

2 lemons

1 orange

½ cup olive oil

1 tablespoon whole-grain mustard

1 teaspoon minced fresh flat-leaf parsley

1 teaspoon minced fresh oregano

½ teaspoon minced fresh chives

2 tablespoons honey

Pinch of red pepper flakes

Kosher salt and ground black pepper

1. Juice the lemons and the orange.

3. Then add the olive oil . . .

5. The herbs . . .

2. Pour the juices into a 16-ounce mason jar . . .

4. The mustard . . .

6. The honey . . .

Mediterranean
Baked Tilapia
(page 282)!

7. The pepper flakes, and salt and black pepper to taste.

8. Screw on the lid and shake the dressing for 45 seconds, to emulsify and get all the flavors going. Store it in the fridge for up to 3 weeks.

WHAT TO DO WITH IT

- *Toss with greens as the base of any salad.*
- *Drizzle over root vegetables before roasting.*
- *Lightly dress quinoa, barley, or rice.*
- *Use as a dressing for pasta salad.*
- *Spoon over sliced grapefruit and oranges for a citrus salad.*
- *Spoon over roasted asparagus.*

THE ERA OF SISTERS!

My sister, Betsy, has lived far away from Oklahoma (Seattle, specifically!) for many years. When she came home for Alex's wedding in 2021, Bets realized how much she loved being back in Oklahoma, and to make a long story short, she now spends 50 percent of her time here! We fixed up a house in town (we call it Sister House) and my girls love to hang there, too. Sisters are a gift at any age, and I cherish every second together!

Caramelized Onions

 35 MINUTES   MAKES 2 HALF-PINT JARS

Happiness is having a jar of caramelized onions in the door of your fridge. The flavor . . . *the flavor* . . . THE FLAVOR! (I'm sorry to shout.) If I had to choose one of the fridge grabs in this chapter and discard the rest forever, well . . . first I would cry because I love them all, but once I dried my tears, I would most definitely choose this one. I hope they find out one day that caramelized onions are the fountain of youth, because if that is the case, I'm gonna live forever!

4 tablespoons (½ stick) salted butter

2 tablespoons olive oil

4 yellow onions, halved and cut into ¼-inch slices

2 teaspoons fresh thyme leaves

6 garlic cloves, minced

2 tablespoons packed brown sugar

¼ teaspoon kosher salt

3. Add the brown sugar and salt . . .

1. In a large skillet, heat the butter and olive oil over medium heat. Add the onions, thyme, and garlic.

4. And continue cooking and stirring until the color is deep and golden, another 8 to 10 minutes.

2. Cook the onions, stirring frequently, until they are golden and starting to caramelize. This is the 20-minute mark!

5. Let the onions cool completely, then divide them between two half-pint jars. Keep refrigerated and use within 1 week.

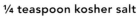

WHAT TO DO WITH THEM

- Warm a small amount in the microwave for 30 seconds, then lay them on top of a burger patty.
- Stir into your favorite mac and cheese.
- Add to any grilled cheese or panini.
- Stir into a mix of sour cream and cream cheese for a delicious caramelized onion dip.
- Add a spoonful to soups or sauces.
- Gift a jar to a friend who loves food!

FUN TIP

For less sweet caramelized onions, omit the brown sugar and instead add ⅛ teaspoon baking soda as you start to cook the onions. It browns 'em fast!

Patty Melts (page 247) come together in a jiffy with a jar of these onions!

PICKLED RED ONIONS

🕐 12 MINUTES (PLUS 1 HOUR TO PICKLE) **MAKES ONE 16-OUNCE JAR**

This oft-used condiment seems to be everywhere these days, and it's easy to see why! Aside from bringing a tangy, yummy, oniony, crunchy finishing touch to a wide range of dishes from nachos to salads, it also delivers the most vibrant shade of pink-purple, which can turn any beige or brown recipe into something much more special. (And much more photogenic, which is why food photographers love these beautiful little delights!) You can buy pickled onions in the grocery store these days, but they're so darn easy to make, you can save yourself the shopping cart space! (You'll need it for that gallon of ice cream you've been on the fence about. I recommend rocky road.)

⅔ cup distilled white vinegar

2 teaspoons sugar

½ teaspoon kosher salt

1 medium red onion, halved and thinly sliced

1. In a small saucepan, combine the vinegar, sugar, salt, and ⅔ cup water. Bring it to a gentle boil.

2. Add the onions and let them simmer for 30 seconds.

3. Transfer the onions to a 16-ounce jar . . .

4. And pour enough liquid over them to cover.

5. Let cool, screw on the lid, then transfer the jar to the fridge.

The onions will be ready within 1 hour, but they will deepen in color and flavor as they sit. Use within 2 weeks.

〰〰〰〰〰〰〰

WHAT TO DO WITH THEM

- *Add a few to the top of tacos.*
- *Sprinkle over any salad.*
- *Add to a roast beef or ham sandwich.*
- *Chop and add to pico de gallo.*
- *Use as a topping for nachos.*
- *Arrange over pizza before or after baking.*
- *Put a dish of them on a charcuterie board.*

I wouldn't dream of making Potato Nachos (page 35) without sprinkling these babies on top!

My favorite salsa on earth!

FIVE-MINUTE SALSA

Salsa is an addictive substance. It's splendid and versatile and magical. And because of that, many folks mistakenly believe that salsa must be cared for and crafted over a long period of time. But it doesn't need to be! No sirree. The truth I have uncovered through my epic adventures with chips and salsa through the years is that the best salsa can actually be made in minutes. *Mere* minutes. *Five* minutes, to be exact. Let that sink in. Actually, let that sink in later! You have some salsa to make.

One 28-ounce can fire-roasted whole tomatoes

One 10-ounce can Ro*tel diced tomatoes and green chiles

1 jalapeño, trimmed and quartered lengthwise

1 garlic clove, minced

¼ teaspoon kosher salt

¼ teaspoon sugar

¼ teaspoon ground cumin

Juice of 1 lime

½ bunch fresh cilantro leaves

Tortilla chips, for testing the salsa (and for serving!)

WHAT TO DO WITH IT

- *Serve with a mix of tortilla chips.*
- *Spoon over nachos, tacos, and enchiladas.*
- *Add to a quesadilla before grilling.*
- *Stir into mac and cheese.*

1. In a food processor or blender, combine the whole tomatoes and Ro*tel.

3. Add the lime juice . . .

5. Pulse until you get the salsa to the consistency you'd like. (I do 10 to 15 pulses so it's uniformly mixed but still a little chunky.)

2. Add the jalapeño, garlic, salt, sugar, and cumin.

4. Then stuff the top with the cilantro. It's impossible to add too much, so don't be shy!

6. Test the seasonings with a tortilla chip and adjust as needed. Store in the fridge for up to 1 week.

REFRIGERATOR PICKLES

⏱ 10 MINUTES (PLUS 8 HOURS TO PICKLE) **MAKES 1 QUART**

My intense love for pickles has grown exponentially through the years. I've always adored them, ever since I was a little girl. To this day I'll eat anything, from a flimsy pickle slice (like the ones in a jar in the back of Grandma Helen's fridge in the '70s) to a crisp, dill-forward, freshly made pickle slice (like the ones in a jar in the front row of my fridge in the 2020s). This is the recipe for the latter, and you will fall in love!

2 English cucumbers

3 tablespoons chopped fresh dill

1 teaspoon mustard seeds

2 green onions, white parts only, thinly sliced

1½ teaspoons kosher salt

⅔ cup white wine vinegar

1. Slice the cucumbers about ⅛ inch thick. (Use a v-slicer or mandoline if you prefer!)

3. Some of the mustard seeds . . .

5. Continue layering the ingredients, pressing and packing everything as you go.

2. In a 1-quart mason jar, layer a few cucumber slices, a little of the dill . . .

4. And a little of the green onion.

6. Add the salt . . .

These will rock your
pickle-loving world!

7. And the vinegar . . .

10. Then turn the jar over a few times to mix.

8. And top it off with cold water until it covers the ingredients.

11. Refrigerate for at least 8 hours before using. Store in the fridge for up to 2 weeks.

9. Screw on the lid tightly . . .

WHAT TO DO WITH THEM

- *Top any burger!*
- *Serve alongside chicken nuggets, hot dogs, or any snack.*
- *Top any salad! Trust me.*
- *Add a little dish to a charcuterie board.*
- *Add to any sandwich.*
- *Chop and add to potato salad, chicken salad, or tuna salad.*

FRIDGE PICKLES VS. REGULAR PICKLES

My husband's late grandmother, Edna Mae, is the person who first showed me just how sublime a homemade pickle could be. Every summer she'd can huge batches of her delicious sweet lime pickles, and to this day I find them impossible to beat. Edna Mae's pickles were made the traditional way, by submerging the filled, sealed jars in simmering water for a time to kill all microorganisms and prepare them for long pantry storage. Water-bath canning, as it's called, is great fun . . . but time-consuming (and equipment-requiring)! So fridge pickles are my jam these days. The temp of the fridge inhibits bacteria growth, and you can just make a jar at a time. Perfect for impatient home . . . canners?

BIG AL'S PICO TOMORROW

⏱ 25 MINUTES (PLUS SEVERAL HOURS TO CHILL) **MAKES 4 CUPS**

Everyone knows how to make pico de gallo. Just combine tomatoes, onions, peppers, lime juice, and cilantro and stir it together . . . and yer done. Or *are* you??? In actuality, truly perfect pico de gallo isn't all that easy to achieve. I didn't realize this until I tasted Al Abeyta's pico de gallo after years of making my own. Al was the dad of close lifelong friends of mine (hi, David and Kash!), and his pico de gallo instantly set the bar for me. The confounding thing is that Al reportedly always used the exact same basic ingredients the rest of us do, but there was just something about his special touch, the way he diced his veggies, and the time he allowed it to sit. Overnight is said to be best, so Al's family took to calling his version "pico tomorrow." It's definitely worth the overnight wait! To this day, I have yet to really do Al's pico tomorrow justice, but I will spend the rest of my life trying.

(Thank you, Al Abeyta! You are loved and you are missed.)

1 medium white onion

2 jalapeños, seeded

6 to 7 medium tomatoes

4 garlic cloves

1½ fistfuls cilantro leaves, minced, plus more to taste

4 pinches kosher salt, plus more to taste

Juice of 3 limes, plus more to taste (see note, though!)

1. Dice the onion, jalapeños, and tomatoes very small. Include some of the jalapeño seeds if you like more heat.

3. Add the cilantro and salt . . .

5. And stir everything together.

2. Combine the veggies in a large bowl, then grate in the garlic using a Microplane zester.

4. Squeeze in the lime juice . . .

6. Wait about 5 minutes, then stir again and taste the mixture with a tortilla chip. Add more salt, lime juice, and cilantro as needed.

7. Cover the bowl with plastic wrap (or add to a large mason jar with a lid) and refrigerate for several hours or overnight.

8. Remove the pico from the fridge and give it a stir. Let it sit for 15 minutes before serving.

WHAT TO DO WITH IT

- *Serve with blue and yellow tortilla chips.*
- *Spoon over tacos.*
- *Put inside a quesadilla with the cheese.*
- *Top a bowl of queso dip.*
- *Pile on a burger.*

TIPS FROM BIG AL'S FAMILY!

- We nicknamed Big Al's Pico de Gallo "Pico Tomorrow" because it is exceptionally better if it sits overnight. If overnight isn't an option, give it as long as you can.

- Don't ever go short on tomatoes.

- Lime juice is optional. It will brighten the flavor if the tomatoes aren't quite there yet.

- The amount of jalapeño depends on the heat. Al bit off the tip to check!

- You figure out when it's right. You may think it needs more red, more white, more green—adjust accordingly.

- Garlic is the real secret. Al didn't tell people about it when he repeated the recipe to those who asked. It kept up demand!

Grandfriends
Day 2019

My favorite condiment
on the planet!

HONEY CHIPOTLE CREMA

⏱ 10 MINUTES **MAKES 1½ CUPS**

I am always a sucker for a creamy/spicy condiment, especially if there's lime and cilantro involved! I just perfectly described this lovely concoction, which could pass as a dressing or a topping or a sauce, depending on your mood! (Or menu.) The small amount of mayo gives this crema a little more body without being too much, and it's such a tasty finishing touch for so many different dishes! Have I mentioned I love this stuff?

1 cup sour cream

½ cup mayonnaise

Grated zest and juice of 1 lime

1 tablespoon honey

1 to 2 heaping tablespoons adobo sauce from a can of chipotle chiles

2 garlic cloves, pressed in a garlic press

¼ cup minced fresh cilantro

Pinch of kosher salt

Pinch of ground black pepper

1. In a medium bowl, combine the sour cream, mayonnaise, and lime zest and juice.

4. And the cilantro, salt, and pepper.

7. Transfer to a 16-ounce jar, screw on the lid, and store in the refrigerator for up to 10 days.

2. Add the honey . . .

5. Stir the mixture . . .

WHAT TO DO WITH IT

- Add a small dollop to the tops of tacos.
- Spread on a cold cut sandwich.
- Spoon over the top of a burger patty.
- Use as a dressing for pasta salad.
- Serve as a topping for roasted vegetables.

3. The adobo and garlic . . .

6. Until the ingredients are combined and the dressing is creamy.

Top Pineapple Chicken Tacos (page 135) with this crema and you will understand its magic.

HEAVENLY MAPLE MUSTARD

🕐 5 MINUTES **MAKES ABOUT 1½ CUPS**

When it comes to this best-of-all-worlds dipping sauce, I don't use the term "heavenly" unadvisedly or lightly. This truly is a blessed combination of otherwise simple and straightforward ingredients, and you'll love how versatile it is as a dip or spread or dressing for so many things! The zip from the mustard, the creaminess from the mayonnaise, the sweetness from the syrup . . . it just works, and the result is not of this world.

½ cup mayonnaise

½ cup grainy brown mustard or Dijon mustard

¼ cup maple syrup

1 teaspoon paprika

½ teaspoon kosher salt

1. In a medium bowl, combine the mayonnaise and mustard.

3. The paprika . . .

5. Stir until everything is mixed together . . .

2. Add the maple syrup . . .

4. And the salt.

6. Then transfer the mixture to a half-pint jar and screw on the lid. Keep refrigerated for up to 2 weeks!

WHAT TO DO WITH IT

- *Use as a dip for chicken strips or chicken nuggets.*
- *Spoon over the top of a bacon cheeseburger.*
- *Use as a dressing for pasta salad.*
- *Use as a dip for French fries or onion rings.*

Try this maple mustard with Pickle Chicken Bites (page 39) and you'll forget about ketchup forever!

This relish gives
softened cream cheese
a new attitude!

QUICK PEPPER RELISH

25 MINUTES **MAKES ONE 16-OUNCE JAR**

I once made this sweet-and-sour relish on my Food Network show as an afterthought. I needed something colorful and fun to spoon over a mundane sausage/hot dog situation, and it turned out to be the surprise of that particular day/week/month! The diced pepper mixture cooks up sticky sweet and almost tastes like candy by the time it's done. Best of all, it's a quick process that results in huge flavor and deliciousness. It's the prettiest, tastiest relish I've ever had! (And I've had lots of relish. The stories I could tell!)

2 tablespoons olive oil

1 small yellow onion, diced small

2 orange bell peppers, diced small

2 jalapeños, seeded and diced small

3 Fresno chiles, seeded and diced small

3 garlic cloves, minced

¾ cup apple cider vinegar

½ cup honey

1 tablespoon mustard seeds

1. In a large skillet, heat the olive oil over medium heat. Add the onion, bell peppers, jalapeños, Fresno chiles, and garlic.

3. Add the vinegar and honey . . .

5. Bring to a gentle boil and cook, stirring occasionally, until the liquid has mostly reduced and the peppers are glossy, 10 to 12 minutes.

2. Stir and cook until the vegetables start to soften, about 4 minutes.

4. Then sprinkle in the mustard seeds.

6. Let the mixture cool, then spoon into a pint jar. Screw on the top and store in the refrigerator for up to 2 weeks.

WHAT TO DO WITH IT

- *Top softened cream cheese (see the photo opposite!) and serve with chips.*
- *Spoon over grilled hot dogs (see Sausage Hoagies with Quick Pepper Relish, page 59).*
- *Serve on top of burgers.*
- *Garnish any submarine sandwich.*

Fun Food

The recipes in this chapter make me smile, because I associate them with good times with my kids. So much of our family food life has centered around the TV for a big football game, or MMA (yes, MMA) event, or basketball championship, or even the latest Marvel movie, and for those occasions there are always lots of appetizers, sandwiches, and other fun-to-eat foods with super-big flavor. Most of it's messy, all of it's tasty, and none of it's fussy in the least. These dishes are great to feed a crowd, which is definitely a factor when all the Drummond kids come home. First, they're all extremely tall. Second, there are several of them. Let's just say they can seriously polish off the grub around here. These recipes are custom designed for teens and young adults . . . and the parents who love them.

So much easier to
eat than wings!

BUFFALO CHICKEN MEATBALLS

⏱ 30 MINUTES **MAKES ABOUT 32 MEATBALLS**

I love the flavor of Buffalo chicken wings, but hate (hate's a strong word and I'm still using it) the whole rigmarole of gnawing them off the bone. The chicken gets stuck in my teeth, the sauce gets all over my mouth and chin, and my fingers wind up a greasy, orangey mess by the time I'm done.

I probably just described the exact reasons why lots of people love eating Buffalo chicken wings, I realize! But these meatballs are more my thing; you can eat 'em with a toothpick or fork, you can celebrate the flavors and sauciness without taking a bath in the stuff, and best of all, they bake in the oven and are ready in less than 30 minutes. No frying (or gnawing or hosing down) required!

1 pound ground chicken

1 garlic clove, minced

2 tablespoons finely diced celery

1 green onion, sliced

⅓ cup plain breadcrumbs

1 large egg

¾ cup plus 1 tablespoon Louisiana-style hot sauce (such as Frank's RedHot)

½ teaspoon kosher salt

½ teaspoon ground black pepper

4 tablespoons (½ stick) butter

FOR SERVING

Celery sticks and leaves

Carrot sticks

Crumbled blue cheese

Peppery Ranch Dressing (page 6) or your favorite ranch or blue cheese dressing

1. Preheat the oven to 400°F. Line a sheet pan with parchment paper.

2. In a large bowl, combine the ground chicken, garlic, celery, green onion, and breadcrumbs.

4. Add 1 tablespoon of the hot sauce, along with the salt and pepper . . .

3. Crack in the egg . . .

5. And stir until everything is combined.

6. Using a tablespoon or small scoop, drop portions of the mixture on the prepared sheet pan.

7. Bake the meatballs until they're cooked through and browned around the edges, about 15 minutes.

8. For the sauce, combine the butter and remaining ¾ cup hot sauce in a deep skillet over medium heat.

9. Heat the mixture until it's just starting to bubble, then turn off the heat.

10. Scrape the baked meatballs into the sauce . . .

11. And toss until they're totally coated.

12. Transfer the meatballs to a platter and pour any extra pan sauce on top. Serve with celery, carrots, blue cheese crumbles, and ranch dressing. Garnish with celery leaves. Have toothpicks nearby!

VARIATIONS

- *Serve with softened tortillas to make wraps.*
- *Serve as an entrée with a side salad.*
- *Cut the meatballs in half and place them on top of pizza before baking.*
- *Make a Buffalo chicken meatball sub!*

POTATO NACHOS

 45 MINUTES **MAKES 4 TO 6 SERVINGS**

I love snacks that can also be a meal! I've made this super-fun potato appetizer for football viewing parties, but it also makes a crazy-good dinner alongside a big green salad. If they're a snack, everyone can dive in with their hands. If I'm serving these for dinner, I'll use a spatula to divvy up individual portions. Either way, the verdict is always the same: *These are so dang good, Mom!!!*

3 pounds unpeeled Yukon Gold potatoes, sliced into ¼-inch-thick rounds

¼ cup olive oil

2 teaspoons kosher salt

1 teaspoon ground black pepper

1 teaspoon garlic powder

Cooking spray

2 cups grated cheddar-Jack cheese

8 slices bacon, cooked and roughly chopped

FOR SERVING

Sour cream

½ cup pickled red onions, homemade (page 14) or store-bought

Sliced green onions

Five-Minute Salsa (page 17)

1. Preheat the oven to 450°F.

2. In a large bowl, place the potatoes, olive oil, salt, pepper, and garlic powder . . .

4. Cover with plastic wrap . . .

6. Mist two sheet pans with cooking spray and spread the potatoes into a single layer on each pan.

3. And toss until everything is well combined.

5. And microwave the potatoes on high for 2 minutes to hasten the cooking process.

7. Bake the potatoes until golden, 12 to 14 minutes.

Page 17!

These are sometimes
called Irish nachos
because of the taters!

8. Dump three-quarters of the potatoes from one of the pans onto the other and gather them in a pile toward the center of the pan.

11. And sprinkle on the rest of the cheese and bacon.

13. To serve, drop dollops of sour cream here and there, add the pickled red onions, and sprinkle on the green onions.

9. Sprinkle three-quarters of the cheese and three-quarters of the bacon on top . . .

12. Return the pan to the oven and bake until the cheese is totally melted, about 5 minutes.

14. Serve with the salsa on the side for dipping!

10. Top with the rest of the potatoes . . .

VARIATIONS

- *Skip the fresh potatoes and use kettle potato chips!*
- *Use cooked taco meat instead of bacon and top with shredded lettuce and diced tomatoes.*
- *Use shredded Buffalo chicken instead of bacon.*
- *Leave off the sour cream and drizzle with Peppery Ranch Dressing (page 6) instead!*

Best chicken nuggets
I've ever tasted!

*Heavenly Maple Mustard
(page 26)!*

PICKLE CHICKEN BITES

⏱ 40 MINUTES   MAKES 4 TO 6 SERVINGS

This is a super-quick, make-at-home version of Chick-fil-A's nuggets, which are tender and tasty because of a slightly weird rumored secret ingredient: pickle juice! This isn't actually a secret at all, as the word got out years ago about how to make the mega-popular fast-food chain's super-amazing, addictive chicken bites. And don't worry—if you aren't a fan of pickles, you can't taste that flavor at all. The pickle juice just serves as a tenderizer/magical touch that will make you fall in love with these chicken bites for life! (By the way, there's also a secret ingredient in the crispy coating that you won't believe. It does amazing things!)

2 pounds boneless, skinless chicken breasts, cut into bite-size chunks

¼ cup juice from a jar of dill pickles

3 tablespoons cornstarch

1 large egg, beaten

1 teaspoon kosher salt, plus more for sprinkling

1 teaspoon ground black pepper

2 cups panko breadcrumbs

1 tablespoon powdered sugar

Vegetable oil, for frying

Heavenly Maple Mustard (page 26), for dipping

1. Put the chicken in a large bowl and pour the pickle juice on top. Toss to combine and let it sit for at least 5 minutes, or up to 20 minutes.

3. Pour in the egg . . .

5. And toss until the chicken is evenly coated.

2. Toss the chicken once more, then sprinkle in the cornstarch.

4. Season with the salt and pepper . . .

6. In a shallow dish or tray, combine the panko and powdered sugar and stir to mix.

7. Add two or three pieces of chicken to the crumbs, coating the whole surface as much as you can. Keep going until all the chicken is breaded.

9. And fry them until they are golden and crisp and the chicken is fully cooked through, carefully moving them around in the oil, 2 to 2½ minutes.

11. And sprinkle with salt.

Repeat to cook the rest of the chicken! Serve with Heavenly Maple Mustard.

8. In a deep skillet or wok, heat 2 inches of oil to 365°F. Gently drop in a few pieces of chicken at a time . . .

10. Use a slotted spoon or spider strainer to remove the chicken to a tray or plate lined with paper towels . . .

VARIATIONS

- *Substitute peeled, deveined jumbo shrimp for the chicken.*
- *Make a fried chicken sub by adding the nuggets to a hoagie roll and topping with coleslaw.*
- *Serve with Honey Chipotle Crema (page 24) or Peppery Ranch Dressing (page 6) instead of the mustard.*

"I always feel like somebody's watchin' me . . ."

PRETZEL DOGS

🕐 35 MINUTES **MAKES 6 PRETZEL DOGS**

Pretzel dogs are an airport delicacy for me, and every time I eat one, I feel instantly transported to LaGuardia Airport, where I first had one many years ago. (I wonder if any cookbook author has ever associated something delicious with LaGuardia Airport? This may be a first.) The truth is, pretzel dogs are so easy to make at home, and the results are even better than what you'll get at LaGuardia! I'm not sure if that is a comfort or not, haha.

You do have to remember to thaw the frozen dinner rolls overnight in the fridge, but once they're thawed out, the process really does move quickly! And the quantity you make is limited only by the number of hot dogs and frozen dinner rolls you have on hand. Great for teenagers and middle-agers alike!

Cooking spray

6 frozen dinner roll dough balls, thawed, at room temperature

6 hot dogs

¼ cup baking soda

1 large egg, beaten

1 teaspoon pretzel salt

Heavenly Maple Mustard (page 26), for serving

Refrigerator Pickles (page 18), for serving

1. Preheat the oven to 425°F. Mist a sheet pan with cooking spray. Bring a 4-quart pot of water to a boil.

2. Roll one dinner roll into a long, skinny roll about twice the length of the hot dogs you're using.

3. Starting at one end and tucking in the open end of the dough to start, coil the dough around the hot dog, being careful not to pull the dough too tight.

4. Leave the end of the hot dog exposed and tuck in the other end of the dough.

5. Repeat to roll up the rest of the hot dogs in dough.

6. Slowly add the baking soda to the boiling water. (Don't add it too fast or the water could boil over. Don't ask me how I know this.)

7. One by one, lower a wrapped hot dog into the water . . .

8. And let it boil for 30 seconds, carefully moving it around the water so that it boils evenly. (If the dough comes loose on one end, no worries! You can fix it after it comes out of the water.)

9. Remove the hot dog to the prepared sheet pan and repeat with the rest.

10. Brush the dough with the beaten egg . . .

11. And sprinkle on some pretzel salt.

12. Bake the pretzel dogs until the surface is deep golden like a pretzel, 10 to 12 minutes.

Serve with Heavenly Maple Mustard and Refrigerator Pickles on the side!

VARIATIONS

- *Use smoked sausage instead of hot dogs.*
- *Use cheddar hot dogs for cheesy pretzel dogs!*

HOMEMADE PRETZEL IDEAS!

If you love soft, luscious, salty pretzels as much as I do, just leave off the hot dogs and use the bread dough to make perfect pretzels in any shape you love! Simply roll the dough into long logs (as in step 2), then form the pretzels and follow the steps on this page to cook and bake. Serve them with cheese sauce, caramel sauce, or even ranch dressing. Once you've gotten used to snacking on a fresh-from-the-oven pretzel, you're going to want to make them weekly! Here are my favorite pretzel shapes:

Pretzel bites: After rolling the dough into long logs, use kitchen shears to snip them into 2-inch pieces.

Pretzel twists: Roll the dough into long logs, then snip each log in half and twist the pieces together. Pinch to seal the ends.

Pretzel hearts: Snip the logs in half and form small hearts. Pinch to seal.

Heavenly Maple Mustard
(page 26)!

My favorite airport snack!

"Rollin', rollin', rollin' . . ."

PULL-APART CHEESEBURGER SLIDERS

⏱ 30 MINUTES **MAKES 12 SANDWICHES**

Packaged Hawaiian rolls are such a staple in our house. They have a long-running association with Sunday communion at our Presbyterian church since the elders often used loaves of store-bought Hawaiian bread in lieu of unleavened wafers, and more than once when they were little, I discovered my kids "playing" communion with torn pieces of rolls I'd originally planned to use for sliders. At least they had Jesus on the brain!

Let's just say these rolls are super versatile—as a dinner roll, as a prop for playtime, or as the basis for all sorts of sandwiches. This pull-apart cheeseburger situation is hands down my favorite way to use them. They're perfect for a family who loves fun food! Or a fun family who loves food. Either one!

(I grew up Episcopalian, so I prefer traditional communion wafers myself . . . but they don't make very good appetizers.)

One 12-count package Hawaiian sweet rolls

3 tablespoons olive oil

½ yellow onion, finely chopped

1¼ pounds ground sirloin

½ teaspoon kosher salt

½ teaspoon ground black pepper

4½ teaspoons Worcestershire sauce

¼ cup mayonnaise

2 tablespoons ketchup

1 tablespoon mustard

8 ounces grated cheddar-Jack cheese

12 dill pickle slices

1 tablespoon everything bagel seasoning

1. Preheat the broiler.

2. Without separating the rolls, use a serrated knife to slice them in half through the middle.

3. Lay the halves cut side up on a sheet pan . . .

4. And broil them until the rolls are lightly toasted, 1½ to 2 minutes. Set aside. Turn the oven to 375°F.

5. In a large skillet over medium-high heat, heat 1 tablespoon of the oil and add the onion. Cook, stirring, until the onion is slightly softened, about 3 minutes.

6. Add the ground beef and sprinkle in the salt and pepper . . .

Such an easy way to make a
bunch of little burgers!

7. Then add the Worcestershire and cook, stirring often, until the meat is done, about 5 minutes. Remove from the heat.

8. In a small bowl, mix the mayonnaise, ketchup, and mustard.

9. Spread the mixture evenly over both halves of the rolls. Now it's time to build!

10. Sprinkle half the cheese in an even layer on the bottom halves of the rolls.

11. Spoon the meat in an even layer all over the cheese . . .

12. Then add the rest of the cheese . . .

13. And center a pickle slice over each roll.

14. Top with the other half of the rolls, brush the surface with the remaining 2 tablespoons olive oil . . .

15. And sprinkle generously with the everything bagel seasoning.

16. Bake until the cheese is melted and the tops of the rolls are toasted, 10 to 12 minutes. Serve immediately and let guests pull 'em apart!

~~~~~~~~~~~~~~~~~~~~~~~~~~~

VARIATIONS

- *Add diced bell pepper to the meat and onion mixture.*
- *Spice it up with red pepper flakes and hot sauce.*
- *Make a taco cheeseburger version! Add taco seasoning to the meat and substitute pepper Jack cheese for the cheddar-Jack.*
- *Make a breakfast version! Swap breakfast sausage for the ground beef and add a layer of scrambled eggs.*

Hot Hawaiian Beef Sandwiches

⏱ 30 MINUTES   MAKES 12 SANDWICHES

It is written: Any type of pull-apart sandwich made with a package of Hawaiian rolls is automatically going to be a hit. Here's another beef-alicious version that's easy to assemble with store-bought roast beef and cheese. You will adore the melty cheesy filling, but especially notable is the tangy, flavorful topping that's baked into the surface of the rolls. Holy moly, these are *good good good*!

One 12-count package Hawaiian sweet rolls

¼ cup mayonnaise or Miracle Whip

Hot sauce

12 thin slices deli roast beef (about ¾ pound)

12 slices pepper Jack cheese

4 tablespoons (½ stick) butter

2 teaspoons lemon pepper

1 tablespoon Dijon mustard

3 to 4 dashes Worcestershire sauce

1. Preheat the oven to 350°F.

2. Without separating them, slice the rolls in half (see step 2, page 46) and place the bottom half in a 9 × 13-inch baking dish.

3. In a small bowl, combine the mayonnaise and hot sauce to taste and stir until smooth.

4. Spread the mixture evenly over the bottom half of the rolls.

5. Lay the roast beef on top of the spread.

6. Lay the cheese slices over the roast beef, overlapping them as you go.

7. Place the other half of the rolls on top and set the pan aside.

8. In a small saucepan, combine the butter, lemon pepper, mustard, and Worcestershire.

10. Then spread it evenly over the tops of the rolls. Yum!

12. Then remove the foil and bake until the tops are deep golden brown, 2 to 3 minutes more. Run a knife between the sandwiches to cut through the slices of beef before serving.

9. Heat the mixture over medium heat until it's melted and bubbly . . .

11. Cover the dish with foil and bake the sandwiches for 12 minutes . . .

VARIATIONS

- *Substitute sliced deli ham for the roast beef.*
- *Make an Italian version by substituting pepperoni, salami, and provolone for the roast beef and pepper Jack.*

My baby, Todd. He's not a baby anymore!

The buttery tops
are amazing!

Totally worth the (social media) hype!

CRISPY ITALIAN MEATBALL WRAP

⏱ 15 MINUTES · **MAKES 1 LARGE WRAP, TO SERVE 1 OR 2**

I may be as old as Methuselah, but since my kids are all teenagers and/or young adults, I'm still basically in my early twenties from a maturity standpoint. As such, I am privy to all of the clever social media recipe trends of late, including this grilled four-quadrant tortilla wrap that took over the Internet a couple of years ago. There's no limit to the combination of meat, cheeses, and veggies you can use, and they really are fun to make with kids! Lately I've been totally crushing on this super-fast Italian version, which uses a top-ten convenience item for me: frozen meatballs! It's nifty, neato, and delicious.

One 12-inch flour tortilla

1 tablespoon prepared pesto

1 tablespoon grated Parmesan cheese

¼ cup baby spinach

1 tablespoon sliced pepperoncini peppers

1 heaping tablespoon marinara sauce

3 frozen store-bought meatballs, thawed and halved (you can thaw in the fridge overnight or in the microwave!)

¼ cup grated mozzarella cheese

2 tablespoons sliced green olives

2 tablespoons butter

1. Every wrap starts the same! Cut a straight line from the center of the tortilla out to the edge.

3. The second wedge is more veggie-centric: Layer the spinach leaves and pepperoncini slices.

5. And lay the halved meatballs on top.

2. Now imagine four wedges! Spread the pesto on one wedge, leaving a slight border, then sprinkle the Parmesan on top.

4. On the next wedge over, spread the marinara, leaving a ½-inch border . . .

6. On the final wedge, sprinkle on the mozzarella and olives.

7. Folding it is the fun part! Picking up the wedge to the left of the cut, fold it over the upper left wedge . . .

8. Then fold the upper left over the upper right . . .

9. And finally the upper right over the bottom right!

10. In a nonstick skillet, heat the butter over medium-low heat. Lay the wrap in the pan, pressing to keep it together.

11. Cook the wrap on both sides, watching to make sure the outside doesn't burn, until the surface is golden and crisp, the cheese is melted, and all the filling is hot. This should take 4 to 5 minutes per side if the heat isn't too high.

12. Remove the wrap to a cutting board and slice it in half through the middle.

13. Enjoy the whole dang thing, or share it with a buddy!

~~~~~~~~~~~~~~~~~~

VARIATIONS

- *Make a chicken/bacon/ranch version with grilled chicken, bacon, Monterey Jack cheese, spinach, and ranch dressing.*
- *Make an Italian cold cut version with pepperoni, salami, mortadella, mozzarella, and Pickled Peppers (page 4).*

Side-view mirror selfie!

SPAGHETTI PIZZA PIE

🕐 30 MINUTES **MAKES 6 TO 8 SERVINGS**

I'm just gonna warn you: This recipe is slightly ridiculous—and by that I mean delicious! It's based on a popular Italian method for using up leftover spaghetti, which I think is so incredibly clever. However, instead of inverting the spaghetti concoction after it's baked, I love to treat the whole thing like a pizza crust and top it with all the good stuff. A conversation starter for sure!

4 large eggs

½ cup grated Parmesan cheese, plus more for serving

1 teaspoon garlic powder

1 teaspoon dried oregano

1 teaspoon red pepper flakes

2¼ cups pizza sauce

Pinch of kosher salt and ground black pepper

8 ounces spaghetti, cooked to al dente and drained (this is a great way to use leftover spaghetti from another meal!)

1½ cups grated mozzarella cheese

1 tablespoon olive oil

1 cup cooked, crumbled sausage (I used store-bought precooked crumbles)

5 thinly sliced green bell pepper rings

¼ cup thinly sliced red onion

¼ cup sliced black olives

Fresh basil leaves, for serving

1. Preheat the oven to 400°F.

2. In a large bowl, whisk the eggs. Add the Parmesan, garlic powder, oregano, pepper flakes, ¼ cup of the pizza sauce, and the salt and black pepper.

4. Add the spaghetti and ½ cup of the mozzarella . . .

6. Heat the olive oil in a 12-inch ovenproof skillet over medium heat. Add the spaghetti mixture . . .

3. Whisk until this crazy-town mixture comes together.

5. And toss it to thoroughly coat the pasta.

7. And spread it evenly out to the edges, flattening the surface somewhat. Reduce the heat to low and let it cook for 2 minutes.

8. Leaving a 1-inch border around the edge as you would a pizza, spread the remaining 2 cups pizza sauce over the spaghetti.

9. Sprinkle on the remaining 1 cup mozzarella . . .

10. The sausage crumbles . . .

11. The green pepper rings and red onion . . .

12. And the black olives. It's starting to look like a pizza!

13. Bake until the cheese is bubbly and the edges are golden and crisp, about 12 minutes. Sprinkle with some more Parmesan and fresh basil leaves, then cut into wedges and serve!

I love it when Paige comes home. (Especially when she cooks dinner!)

A brilliant pasta/
pizza combo!

Page 29!

Better than any stadium dog
(and stadium dogs are darn good!).

SAUSAGE HOAGIES WITH QUICK PEPPER RELISH

⏱ 15 MINUTES **MAKES 4 HOAGIES**

Anything resembling a hot dog is always super fun to make (and eat!), and this version is, I imagine, what every basic hot dog dreams of becoming one day. Smoked sausage adds flavor and richness, and the quick pepper relish adds a tangy sweetness that will make all pickle relish you've had in your life pale in comparison! These are perfect for game days in front of the TV, and they'll make you glad you didn't brave the stadium crowds. Stadium hot dogs have their place in the world, of course . . . but these are a whole other level.

You can either grab the pepper relish from the fridge or just make it in real time to use in this recipe. It comes together quickly and is delicious either way!

4 tablespoons (½ stick) butter	**4 jalapeño smoked sausage links**	**Green leaf lettuce**
4 hoagie rolls, split	**½ cup mayonnaise**	**Quick Pepper Relish (page 29), for serving**

1. Heat a griddle over medium heat and coat it with the butter. Place the rolls cut side down and grill them until golden brown. Set the rolls aside and increase the heat under the griddle to medium.

2. Slice the sausages down the middle . . .

3. Place them cut side down on the griddle . . .

4. And cook them until browned, about 4 minutes per side.

5. Remove them to a plate.

6. To make one sandwich, spread both halves of a roll with mayonnaise and add a lettuce leaf or two.

7. Add two halves of a sausage link . . .

8. And spoon on a generous portion of the relish! Repeat to make the rest of the hoagies.

VARIATIONS

- *Lay a piece of provolone on the cut side of the sausage after flipping it.*
- *Use any hot dog or smoked sausage!*

These boots were made for . . . getting dirtier and dirtier!

CHEESY CALZONES

⏱ 50 MINUTES · MAKES 8 CALZONES

I almost didn't include this recipe in this book, because I worried that you would consider calzones a little basic or boring, and that you'd yawn and say, "Been there, done that!"—and in the life of a middle child like me, that is pretty much a worst-case scenario. However, I decided to push through my FOBB (Fear of Being Boring) and share it anyway, because these really are *exactly* what calzones are meant to be. The crust is golden, the filling is cheesy and flavorful, and the result is something special. (And have I mentioned not boring?)

I use my go-to pizza crust, which I usually have hanging out in the fridge, for a time-saver. But feel free to use everything from thawed frozen dinner rolls to basic crescent roll dough from the supermarket! All shortcut doughs and crusts are allowed!

Pizza dough for 1 pizza (about 1 pound), homemade (page 208) or store-bought

1½ cups ricotta cheese

¼ cup roughly chopped fresh flat-leaf parsley

Kosher salt and ground black pepper

4 or 5 cloves Garlic Confit (optional; page 3)

Flour, for dusting the surface

8 slices provolone cheese

½ cup grated mozzarella cheese

2 large egg yolks

2 tablespoons heavy cream

1¼ cups grated Parmesan cheese

Warmed marinara sauce, for serving

1. Preheat the oven to 475°F.

2. Divide the dough into 8 equal portions . . .

3. And roll each piece into a ball.

4. In a medium bowl, place the ricotta, parsley, and a pinch of salt and pepper. Add the garlic confit (if using) and stir to combine.

5. Lightly flour a flat work surface and roll out one of the balls of dough until super thin, about 6 to 7 inches.

6. Tear a piece of provolone in half and place the pieces on the bottom half of the dough round.

7. Spoon about 2 tablespoons of the ricotta filling on top of the cheese . . .

8. Then top the ricotta with 1 tablespoon of mozzarella.

9. Grab the top half of the dough round . . .

10. And fold it over the filling, meeting up the edges with the bottom half.

11. Lightly press to distribute the filling a little more, making sure to gently press out any air bubbles inside.

12. Pleat the edge by rolling the edge over itself, pressing at the end to seal.

13. Repeat to make the rest of the calzones, transferring them to a sheet pan as you finish. Use a knife to make three cuts in the top of each calzone.

14. In a small bowl, whisk the eggs and cream . . .

15. Then generously brush the surface of the calzones on the top and around the sides.

16. Sprinkle the tops with grated Parmesan.

17. Bake the calzones until deep golden brown, 12 to 14 minutes. Serve with marinara sauce!

~~~~~~~~~~~~~~~~~~~~~~~~~~~~~~~~~~

VARIATIONS

- *Add cooked crumbled Italian sausage to the ricotta mixture.*
- *Layer sliced pepperoni over the ricotta mixture inside each calzone.*
- *Add any pizza toppings you like: sliced black olives, thinly sliced red onion, diced bell pepper, and so forth!*

Basic calzone is anything but basic!

Mostly Meatless

As the spouse/sweetie pie of a cattle rancher, it may seem a little odd for me to utter, write, or even *think* the word "meatless"—let alone devote an entire chapter of this cookbook to noncarnivorous recipes. But I used to be a vegetarian in my pre-Ladd days, so hear me out: These recipes celebrate all the wonderful nonmeaty things in life, from vegetables to noodles to pastry to eggs to cheese! Note that, as the title specifies, these are *mostly* meatless ideas: I suggest ways to add a protein here and there (and you'll even find a small amount of pancetta in one of the dishes!), so you can pick and choose, depending on your preferences. As meatless chapters go, consider this one the least strict of all time, and use the recipes as a canvas for your own creative add-ons.

VEGGIE RAGÙ WITH CHEESY POLENTA

⏱ 35 MINUTES **MAKES 6 TO 8 SERVINGS**

This is my favorite way to cook and eat: Make some kind of chunky, hearty stew, pair it with some kind of creamy starch, and let everyone serve themselves. Forget the salad! Forget the bread! Neither is necessary with this polenta-and-ragù combo. It is hearty and so satisfying, and it's just as perfect for company as it is just for you and your sweetie. Or you and your babies. Or just you! (It keeps really nicely in the fridge for a few days, so go ahead and make the whole portion even if it's just for yourself!)

3 cups low-sodium vegetable broth, plus more as needed

2 tablespoons olive oil

4 tablespoons (½ stick) butter

1 medium eggplant, cut into ½-inch cubes

1 yellow or white onion, halved and thinly sliced

1 medium zucchini, diced

1 red bell pepper, diced

5 garlic cloves, minced

1 tablespoon Italian seasoning

Kosher salt and ground black pepper

1 heaping tablespoon tomato paste

One 28-ounce can whole tomatoes

1 teaspoon garlic powder

1 teaspoon onion powder

1 cup instant polenta

⅓ cup grated Parmesan cheese, plus more for serving

Fresh basil, for garnish

1. Pour the broth into a medium saucepan and turn the heat to low.

3. And cook, stirring constantly, until the onion starts to soften, about 3 minutes.

5. Stir and cook for a minute . . .

2. Heat the olive oil and 2 tablespoons of the butter in a large high-sided skillet over medium-high heat. Add the eggplant and onion . . .

4. Add the zucchini, bell pepper, garlic, Italian seasoning, and a pinch of salt and pepper.

6. Then add the tomato paste and cook, stirring, for another minute.

Ragù + Polenta = Heaven

7. Crushing them by hand, add the tomatoes and their juice . . .

10. Add the polenta, whisking constantly . . .

14. To serve, spoon a bed of polenta into a wide shallow bowl.

8. And stir to combine. Reduce the heat to low and simmer for 15 minutes, stirring occasionally.

11. Until it's all incorporated. Reduce the heat to low.

15. Top with a generous portion of the ragù. Sprinkle with a little Parmesan and garnish with fresh basil leaves.

9. While the ragù is simmering, make the polenta. Add the garlic powder and onion powder to the broth, then increase the heat to medium-high and bring the broth to a gentle boil.

12. Add the remaining 2 tablespoons butter, the Parmesan, and a pinch of salt and pepper . . .

13. And stir until the butter is melted and the Parmesan is totally incorporated. Splash in a little extra broth as needed for consistency. Remove from the heat.

VARIATIONS

- *Serve the ragù over mashed potatoes.*
- *Serve the ragù over cheese grits.*
- *Stir cheddar or Monterey Jack cheese into the polenta.*
- *Add diced mushrooms to the vegetable mixture.*
- *Add ⅓ cup heavy cream to the ragù toward the end of the cooking.*

MUSHROOM SWISS LETTUCE WRAPS

🕐 25 MINUTES **MAKES 4 SERVINGS**

I haven't said this phrase in quite a while, so this is as good a time as any to break it out: This recipe makes my skirt fly up! Sorry, but it's true. The dark, delicious mushrooms, the melty, creamy Swiss, the cool, crisp leaves of romaine . . . my gosh! I could eat these lettuce wraps every day for the rest of my life.

(I'll just make a note to wear pants when I do.)

4 large portobello mushrooms

2 tablespoons soy sauce

2 tablespoons balsamic vinegar

1 teaspoon garlic powder

1 teaspoon dried oregano

Ground black pepper

1 teaspoon olive oil

1 red bell pepper, sliced into strips

1 small yellow onion, halved and sliced

4 slices Swiss cheese

Minced fresh chives or sliced green onions, for garnish

1 head baby romaine or romaine hearts, separated into leaves

1. Use a spoon to scrape out the gills and remove the stems on the underside of the mushrooms . . .

3. In a small pitcher or bowl, combine the soy sauce, balsamic vinegar, garlic powder, oregano, and a pinch of black pepper . . .

5. Heat the olive oil in a large nonstick pan over medium heat. Add the mushrooms, bell pepper, and onion . . .

2. Then slice them into strips.

4. And stir it with a fork.

6. And pour in the sauce.

The mushroom-pepper combo is marvelous!

7. Toss the veggies in the sauce and cook them, stirring frequently . . .

9. Reduce the heat to low, then overlap the cheese slices on top of the mushroom mixture . . .

11. Sprinkle the chives on top and turn off the heat. Serve with lettuce leaves and let everyone spoon the mushroom mixture on individual leaves.

8. Until most of the liquid has been cooked off and the mushrooms and the veggies are nicely browned, 10 to 12 minutes.

10. And put the lid (or sheet pan) on the pan to let the cheese melt, 1 to 2 minutes.

VARIATIONS

- *Substitute zucchini or eggplant for the mushrooms.*
- *Add chopped artichoke hearts to the vegetables.*
- *Spoon the mushroom mixture onto sourdough toast.*

Ladd, Red, and Rusty!

WHITE BEANS AND GREENS

⏱ 40 MINUTES **MAKES 6 SERVINGS**

Eating this delightful cross between a soup and a stew will make you feel like you have accomplished something in your life. At least for that day. First of all, it's hearty and comforting. Second, it could be argued that it's pretty healthy! Third, it's a super-speedy thing to pull together. Fourth, you can make the (absolutely addictive) croutons while the pot is simmering, so they don't add any extra time to the process! Fifth, the croutons are doused in butter before they're baked, so that might negate my second point above about it being pretty healthy.

Ninth, I've totally lost count . . . so just scratch everything I said and make this incredibly delicious meal right now!

4 ounces chopped pancetta

1 medium onion, medium-diced

1 large carrot, peeled and medium-diced

1 celery stalk, medium-diced

4 garlic cloves, minced

2 teaspoons minced fresh thyme

2 teaspoons minced fresh oregano, plus more for garnish

Kosher salt and ground black pepper

½ cup white wine (or low-sodium chicken or vegetable broth)

4 cups low-sodium chicken or vegetable broth

Two 15-ounce cans cannellini beans, drained and rinsed

2 cups thinly sliced hearty greens (such as kale or collards), stems removed

1 small loaf sourdough or ciabatta bread

3 tablespoons butter, melted

Grated white cheddar cheese, for serving

Red pepper flakes, for serving

1. Preheat the oven to 400°F.

2. Heat a large pan over medium-high heat, then add the pancetta if you'd like.

4. Remove the pancetta and set it aside.

6. Stir and cook the vegetables until softened, about 5 minutes.

3. Cook it for a few minutes, until the fat is mostly rendered and the pancetta is slightly crisp.

5. Add the onion, carrot, celery, garlic, thyme, oregano, and a pinch of salt and pepper to the pan.

7. Add the wine, scraping the pan to deglaze as you go.

A bowlful of goodness right here!

8. Simmer for a few minutes to let the wine reduce by about half . . .

9. Then add the broth!

10. Dump in the beans . . .

11. And the greens!

12. Stir, bring the mixture to a boil, and reduce the heat to low. Simmer for 10 minutes while you make the croutons.

13. Tear the bread into chunks and place them on a sheet pan.

14. Pour the melted butter on top, sprinkle with salt and pepper . . .

15. And toss with your hands to coat. Bake the croutons for 7 to 8 minutes . . .

16. Until they're golden and crisp around the edges. (Again, these are addictive!)

17. Taste the beans and adjust the salt and pepper . . .

18. Then dish it up in a bowl. Sprinkle on a little cheddar, some fresh oregano, pepper flakes, and a few pieces of cooked pancetta.

19. Add croutons to the top and dive in!

VARIATIONS

- Use bacon or diced ham instead of pancetta.
- Add diced mushrooms with the onion, carrot, and celery.
- Use canned pinto beans instead of cannellini.

PUFF PASTRY QUICHE

1 HOUR 15 MINUTES **MAKES 6 TO 8 SERVINGS**

Quiche is perfectly permissible to serve morning, noon, and night, and I am so grateful to have discovered this easy puff pastry version, which can easily be adapted with whatever filling you feel like using. I love grabbing my jar of Caramelized Onions from the fridge to deepen the flavors, and you can add anything from diced ham to mushrooms. If it can go in an omelet, it can go in this quiche! (BTW, I love quiche for dinner. It's a thing around here.)

2 tablespoons olive oil

1 small bunch Swiss chard, stems removed, leaves coarsely chopped (about 4 cups)

Kosher salt and ground black pepper

One 17.3-ounce package (2 sheets) frozen puff pastry, thawed in the fridge overnight

9 large eggs

¾ cup sour cream

1½ cups half-and-half

2 cups grated pepper Jack cheese

½ cup Caramelized Onions (page 12)

1 cup multicolored cherry tomatoes, halved

5 dill sprigs

1. Preheat the oven to 375°F.

2. Heat the olive oil in a medium skillet over medium-high heat. Add the Swiss chard and a pinch of salt and pepper . . .

4. Lay one sheet of the puff pastry in one side of a 9 × 13-inch baking dish, pressing and stretching to make the dough come up the sides.

6. Press the seam firmly to seal the dough as much as possible.

3. And cook until the chard starts to wilt, about 1 minute. It will shrink quite a bit! Remove it from the heat.

5. Lay the second sheet of pastry in the other side of the dish, overlapping the first sheet in the middle. Press the pastry around the edges and bring the dough up the sides.

7. Crack the eggs into a pitcher and add the sour cream . . .

Perfect for breakfast,
lunch, or dinner!

8. The half-and-half, and a pinch of salt and pepper . . .

12. Add the Swiss chard in a single layer . . .

16. And arrange the dill sprigs in the gaps here and there.

9. And whisk until well combined. Set aside.

13. Then sprinkle on the rest of the cheese . . .

17. Cover the dish with foil and bake for 20 minutes. Remove the foil and bake until the crust around the edges is golden, 20 to 25 minutes longer. Let it sit for 10 minutes before cutting into squares to serve.

10. Sprinkle two-thirds of the pepper Jack all over the surface of the puff pastry . . .

14. And pour the egg mixture on top.

VARIATIONS

- *To save even more time, skip the sauté step for the chard! Just chop the greens smaller and add them straight to the quiche in the order directed.*
- *Substitute fresh spinach for the chard.*
- *Add crumbled goat cheese on top of the grated cheese.*
- *Add chopped roasted red peppers along with the onions.*

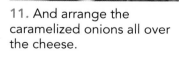

11. And arrange the caramelized onions all over the cheese.

15. Arrange the tomatoes evenly over the surface, cut side up . . .

TEA KETTLE SOUP

🕐 15 MINUTES   **MAKES 1 OR 2 SERVINGS**

The funny name for this soup can be a little confusing, so to set the record straight: This soup is not made in a tea kettle! It's made straight in the bowl it's served in, and the tea kettle merely serves the purpose of getting the boiling water into the bowl. This lightning-fast soup is nothing more than another approach to doctored-up ramen, but it happens to be my absolute favorite combination of add-ins. (Why are straw mushrooms so mysteriously, weirdly wonderful?!?) It also happens to be super quick (it takes only 15 minutes) and super easy (you don't have to drag out a saucepan!), so get ready to slurp away!

This makes a big ol' bowl of soup, so feel free to share with another noodle lover in your life!

1 package chicken-flavored ramen (or whatever flavor you like!)

1 tablespoon sriracha, plus more to taste

¼ cup shredded carrots

1 green onion, sliced

¼ cup canned straw mushrooms or regular canned mushrooms, drained

4 ears canned baby corn

1 tablespoon soy sauce

Juice of ½ lime

2 tablespoons chopped salted roasted peanuts

1. In a tea kettle or small saucepan, bring 2½ cups water to a boil.

2. Unwrap the ramen package and sprinkle the chicken seasoning in a large soup or pasta bowl.

4. Then lay the noodles on top.

6. Add the mushrooms (if you have a full-size can, pop the extras in a ziptop bag and keep them in the fridge!).

3. Squirt in the sriracha . . .

5. Sprinkle on the carrots and green onion . . .

7. Cut each baby corn ear into 3 pieces and add them to the bowl . . .

Just add water!

8. Then add the soy sauce.

10. After 4 minutes, squeeze in the lime juice . . .

12. Sprinkle on the peanuts and dig in!

9. Very slowly pour in the boiling water, making sure you pour it over all the ingredients. Let the ingredients sit for 4 minutes without stirring.

11. Then break up the noodles and gently stir the soup. Make sure the sriracha is well incorporated.

VARIATIONS

* Add fresh cilantro leaves just before serving.
* Add chopped cashews or almonds instead of peanuts.
* Add a sprinkle of red pepper flakes before adding the boiling water, for a little more heat.
* Add chopped canned water chestnuts before adding the boiling water.

Head tilt alert!

CURRIED PUMPKIN SOUP

 35 MINUTES **MAKES 6 TO 8 SERVINGS**

I was well into my forties before I finally discovered that the phrase is "toe the line" and not "tow the line," and I was also well into my forties before I finally discovered that canned pumpkin puree is as much a savory ingredient as a sweet one! It takes me a while sometimes. Life is hard.

Once you discover how incredible canned pumpkin is, it will unlock a world of possibilities, from ravioli stuffing to savory breads to this incredibly fast soup with an herby pumpkin seed topping. It's one of the fastest recipes in this book, and it's also one of the most surprisingly delicious! Serve it to friends on a casual fall Friday night. They'll hug you for it!

4 tablespoons olive oil

1 large yellow onion, halved and thinly sliced

4 garlic cloves, minced

2 tablespoons minced fresh ginger

1 mounded tablespoon curry powder

Kosher salt and ground black pepper

Two 15-ounce cans pumpkin puree (psst—not pumpkin pie filling!)

3 cups low-sodium vegetable broth

1 cup canned full-fat coconut milk

1 tablespoon packed brown sugar

¼ teaspoon ground cinnamon

1 cup pepitas

½ teaspoon ground cumin

½ teaspoon garlic powder

¼ cup chopped fresh cilantro

¼ cup chopped fresh flat-leaf parsley

1. Heat 3 tablespoons of the olive oil in a large heavy-bottomed pot over medium heat. Add the onion, garlic, and ginger . . .

3. Sprinkle in the curry powder along with a pinch of salt and pepper . . .

5. Add the wonderfully weird pumpkin! (Just to reiterate: This is not pumpkin pie filling, which is spiced and sweetened. It's just plain ol' pumpkin.)

2. And cook for 2 minutes so the flavors are released and the onion begins to soften.

4. And cook, stirring constantly, for another couple of minutes.

6. Stir it in with the onion . . .

The secret's in
the pumpkin!

7. Then add the broth . . .

8. The coconut milk . . .

9. And the brown sugar and cinnamon.

10. Stir to combine and bring to a gentle boil. Reduce the heat and simmer for 10 minutes while you make the topping.

11. Pour the pepitas into a dry skillet over medium heat . . .

12. And lightly toss them as they toast, 3 to 4 minutes, taking care to not let them burn.

13. Pour the pepitas into a bowl and add the cumin, garlic powder, a pinch of salt, the cilantro, and the parsley.

14. Stir the pepita mixture, drizzling in the remaining 1 tablespoon olive oil.

15. Stir the soup and add more salt if it needs it! You don't want the soup to be overly sweet.

16. Dish up the soup and add a generous topping of the herby pepitas!

VARIATIONS

- *Use roasted butternut squash instead of pumpkin. Use a potato masher or immersion blender to puree the squash.*
- *Substitute half-and-half for the coconut milk.*
- *Stir ¼ cup pesto into the soup while it simmers.*
- *Add a spoonful of sour cream or plain Greek yogurt to the top for serving.*
- *Top with cooked crumbled bacon or pancetta.*

Made with fresh tomatoes!

GRILLED CHEESE AND BROILED TOMATO SOUP

🕐 30 MINUTES **MAKES 2 SERVINGS**

Tomato soup and grilled cheese is the most wholesome and perfect comfort food combination in modern history, and this is a quick and easy way to get tomato soup on the table in a very short window of time. Equipment-wise, the broiler and blender are the stars of the show, and you can make the very cheese-tastic sandwich while the soup ingredients are in the oven. *Soup in a blender . . . it has a nice ring to it if you ask me!*

10 ounces grape or cherry tomatoes

2 tablespoons tomato paste

3 green onions, sliced

3 garlic cloves, minced

Kosher salt and ground black pepper

2 tablespoons olive oil

½ cup heavy cream

1 rosemary sprig

1 tablespoon balsamic vinegar

2 tablespoons pesto

2 slices Jewish rye and pumpernickel deli swirl bread

4 thin slices American or cheddar cheese

3 ounces Gruyère cheese, grated

2 tablespoons mayonnaise

2 tablespoons butter

1. Preheat the broiler.

2. Combine the tomatoes and tomato paste in a 2-quart baking dish.

4. And the olive oil . . .

6. Place the dish under the broiler for 5 to 6 minutes to lightly char the tomatoes. They should burst and the skins should start to pull away.

3. Add the green onions, garlic, a pinch of salt and pepper . . .

5. And mix well.

7. Remove from oven and immediately add the heavy cream . . .

8. And the rosemary and balsamic.

9. Toss everything together . . .

10. And broil for another 6 minutes, until the cream has reduced and thickened slightly. Remove the pan from the oven and set aside.

11. Spread the pesto over both pieces of bread.

12. Overlap 2 slices of American or cheddar cheese on each slice of bread.

13. Add the Gruyère on one half.

14. Place the second slice of bread on top and smear the top with 1 tablespoon of the mayonnaise.

15. Heat a medium cast-iron skillet or griddle over medium-low heat and melt the butter. Add the sandwich, mayonnaise side down. Smear the remaining 1 tablespoon of mayonnaise on the top.

16. Toast the sandwich until the bottom slice of bread is golden and the cheese is starting to melt (you can put a lid on the skillet to hasten this along!), then flip it over to the other side and toast until the cheese is fully melted. Remove the sandwich from the heat.

VARIATIONS

- *Substitute chopped red bell pepper for some of the tomatoes for a nice tomato-pepper flavor.*
- *Add 1 teaspoon red pepper flakes to the tomatoes to give the soup a nice spice.*
- *Substitute any bread and cheese you'd like in the grilled cheese.*

17. Pour the tomato mixture into a blender, discarding the rosemary sprig . . .

18. And pulse 2 to 3 times, just to break it up. (Note: Do not turn the blender on full speed, as blending hot ingredients can be dangerous!)

19. Divide the soup between two bowls . . .

20. Then slice the sandwich in half and share!

MEET MY GRANDSON, GEORGE!

Alex and Mauricio had a baby! A baby Golden Retriever, to be specific. His name is George, and he's basically the cutest dude in the universe. He lives with his mom and dad in Dallas, so he's a total city dog in many ways, but he likes coming to visit his canine aunts and uncles on the ranch. We love you, George!

A staple of my
Gen X childhood!

ONE-POT HOMEMADE O'S

⏱ 35 MINUTES **MAKES 6 TO 8 SERVINGS**

Of all the childhood convenience food delights in my memory—and there are many, as I am a proud, preservative-raised member of Gen X—SpaghettiOs are definitely in the top ten. To this day, I would not hesitate for one second to crack open a can and eat a bowl all by myself . . . watching *Gilligan's Island* on a damask sofa, preferably! (And wearing Love's Baby Soft perfume and waiting for Steve-O to call . . .)

This one-pan, from-scratch re-creation of the original canned delicacy is a delicious dead-ringer. While it'll never quite live up to the original, I think it's worthy of becoming a new family favorite, no matter what generation you're a card-carrying member of!

3 tablespoons olive oil

1 large onion, finely diced

4 garlic cloves, minced

1 tablespoon minced fresh rosemary

6 tablespoons tomato paste

4 cups low-sodium chicken or vegetable broth, plus more as needed

½ cup half-and-half

1 teaspoon paprika

½ teaspoon chili powder

¼ teaspoon cayenne pepper

Pinch of kosher salt, plus more to taste

12 ounces uncooked anelletti (ring) pasta

¼ cup grated Parmesan cheese, plus more for serving

Minced fresh flat-leaf parsley, for serving

1. Heat the oil in a deep skillet over medium-high heat. Add the onion, garlic, and rosemary . . .

3. Add the tomato paste . . .

5. Add the broth, stirring constantly . . .

2. And cook, stirring often, for 2 minutes until the onion begins to soften.

4. And stir, cooking the mixture for an additional minute.

6. And the half-and-half.

7. Stir to combine, then add the paprika, chili powder, cayenne, and salt.

8. Stir and bring the mixture to a gentle boil . . .

9. Then add the cute pasta circles! The pasta cooks in the sauce, so no need to boil it separately!

10. Stir in the pasta, reduce the heat to low, and let the mixture cook, stirring frequently, for 10 to 12 minutes . . .

11. Until the pasta is cooked and most of the liquid is absorbed. Add a little more broth if needed toward the end of the cooking process, if the pasta needs a little more time.

12. Turn off the heat and stir in the Parmesan.

13. Dish it up immediately and sprinkle on more Parmesan and some parsley.

VARIATIONS

- Use elbow macaroni, corkscrew pasta, or farfalle.
- Stir in cooked broccoli florets right before serving.
- Top each bowl with sliced grilled chicken.

CHEESY O'S

25 MINUTES **MAKES 6 TO 8 SERVINGS**

I remember back in my SpaghettiOs days, I always thought a cheesy version of the original canned delight would be so amazing. I'm not sure whether they ever tried to release such a product (if they did, it never made its way to Landers Brothers grocery store in Bartlesville, Oklahoma), but the good news is that I'm a grown-up now and get to make childhood food fantasies come to life whenever I want! What a dreamy recipe this is—perfect as a side dish or main course. You are sure to fall in love.

12 ounces anelletti (ring) pasta

3 tablespoons butter

2 tablespoons olive oil

1 small yellow onion, medium-diced

3 garlic cloves, minced

3 tablespoons all-purpose flour

2½ cups whole milk

½ cup heavy cream

Kosher salt and ground black pepper

4 ounces white Velveeta, cut into large chunks

1 cup grated Monterey Jack cheese

1 cup grated Havarti cheese

Minced fresh flat-leaf parsley, for serving

1. Cook the pasta in a large pot of boiling water according to the package directions. Drain and set aside.

2. While the pasta is boiling, in a large deep skillet, melt the butter with the olive oil over medium heat. Add the onion and garlic . . .

3. And stir and cook until they're softened, 3 to 4 minutes.

4. Sprinkle the flour on top . . .

5. And cook, stirring, until light golden, about 1 minute.

6. Add the milk and cream . . .

7. And a generous pinch of salt and pepper . . .

My new favorite
mac and cheese!

8. And cook the mixture, stirring often, until it's thick and bubbling, 3 to 4 minutes.

10. And stir until the sauce is melted and luscious. Taste and adjust the salt and pepper.

12. Then stir until the pasta is totally coated in the luscious cheese!

9. Reduce the heat to low, add all of the cheeses . . .

11. Turn off the heat and add the pasta . . .

13. Dish it up and serve immediately, with a sprinkle of parsley on each serving.

VARIATIONS

- *Use elbow macaroni, corkscrew pasta, or farfalle.*
- *Cook sliced mushrooms with the onions.*
- *Stir in cooked broccoli florets right before serving.*
- *Top each bowl with sliced grilled chicken.*

Early-morning Fred. (He hasn't had his coffee yet.)

Pasta for President!

Anyone who's lived on this earth for fifty-plus years has seen many a food trend come and go, and the one that probably concerned me the most (thank goodness it's waning, from what I can see!) was the era of pasta malignment! The low-carb emphasis in recent decades somehow caused pasta to become a dietary scapegoat . . . but rest assured, I was there all along, slurping spaghetti while continuing to sing its praises! I've loved pasta all my life, after all. From buttered egg noodles to tagliatelle with truffles, I can't imagine living in a world without it!

While pasta is not an everyday indulgence for me, it certainly makes a weekly appearance on Drummond family plates. Here are some new noodle favorites!

ONE-PAN GNOCCHI WITH SAUSAGE AND CAULIFLOWER

30 MINUTES · **MAKES 6 TO 8 SERVINGS**

Lord have mercy, this recipe is good. It's rich and hearty and creamy and dreamy and seriously luscious . . . and it comes together pretty darn quick thanks to tender store-bought gnocchi. Everything cooks in one pan, which means you don't even have to pre-cook the gnocchi. That's a pan savings of 50 percent! (I sound like an infomercial personality!) Anyway, this is a recipe you can decide to make at the last minute, and it'll still taste like something you crafted with care. So yummy!

2 tablespoons olive oil

1 pound spicy Italian sausage links, casings removed

1 medium onion, halved and sliced

4 garlic cloves, minced

1 head cauliflower, broken into small and medium florets

2 tablespoons tomato paste

Kosher salt and ground black pepper

½ cup red wine (or chicken broth)

2½ cups low-sodium chicken broth

One 15-ounce can tomato sauce

2 heaping tablespoons prepared pesto

One 15-ounce package shelf-stable gnocchi

4 ounces cream cheese, at room temperature (or you can microwave it for 25 seconds to soften)

3 cups baby kale

½ cup grated Parmesan cheese, for serving

Fresh basil leaves, for garnish

1. Heat the olive oil in a large deep skillet or Dutch oven over medium-high heat. Add chunks of the sausage in a single layer and cook for 3 minutes on the first side . . .

2. Then flip them over and let them finish cooking on the other side.

4. Add the onion, garlic, and cauliflower . . .

3. Remove the sausage from the pan and set it aside.

5. And cook, stirring frequently, for 3 minutes.

A wondrous
one-pan masterpiece!

6. Add the tomato paste and a pinch of salt and pepper and stir to coat the veggies. Let them cook for 1 minute . . .

7. Then add the red wine . . .

8. The chicken broth . . .

9. The tomato sauce . . .

10. And the pesto.

11. Stir, then add the gnocchi and the cooked sausage.

12. Reduce the heat to low and cook, stirring frequently, until the gnocchi are tender and the sauce has thickened, 6 to 7 minutes.

13. Add the cream cheese . . .

14. And stir until it's melted, about 2 minutes.

15. Turn off the heat, add the baby kale . . .

16. And stir it until it's wilted, about 2 minutes! Taste and add more salt and pepper if needed. Serve with a sprinkle of Parmesan and torn basil leaves.

ROASTED BROCCOLI AND CAULIFLOWER PASTA

⏱ 30 MINUTES **MAKES 4 TO 6 SERVINGS**

Oven pasta sauces are an even newer concept for me than one-pan pastas, and I have fallen in love with them. The idea is to cook a simple pasta sauce in a baking dish in the oven, then toss cooked pasta into the dish when the sauce is done. I've discovered that the broiler unleashes so many different dimensions of flavor than a regular skillet does, and it's so much easier to stick a dish in the oven than to babysit a sauce on the stove. If you've never tried an oven pasta sauce, this is the perfect port of entry. All aboard!

Kosher salt

12 ounces orecchiette

1 head broccoli, broken into small and medium florets

1 head cauliflower, broken into small and medium florets

1 small onion, diced

4 garlic cloves, minced

3 tablespoons olive oil

Ground black pepper

1 cup heavy cream

½ cup low-sodium chicken broth

3 tablespoons butter, cut into pats

¾ cup pine nuts

½ cup prepared pesto, plus more for serving

¾ cup grated Parmesan cheese

1. Preheat the broiler.

2. Bring a pot of lightly salted water to a boil and pour in the pasta to cook according to the package directions.

GET A PASTA POT!

A strainer/pot combo means you can drain your pasta right at the stove. It saves time and steps, and you'll have the pasta water to thin your sauce!

3. Meanwhile, combine the broccoli, cauliflower, onion, and garlic in a 9 × 13-inch ovenproof baking dish. Pour the olive oil on top and add a pinch of salt and pepper.

4. Pour in the cream . . .

5. And the broth.

6. Then stir everything together and top with the pats of butter. Place on the middle rack under the broiler until the vegetables are roasted and slightly browned around the edges, 8 to 10 minutes. Watch that the veggies don't burn!

7. While the veggies are broiling, add the pine nuts to a small dry skillet over medium heat . . .

8. And toast them, shaking the pan, until they turn golden, 2 to 3 minutes. Be careful not to burn them! Remove them from the heat.

9. The veggies are ready! Remove them from the oven . . .

10. And immediately pour the drained pasta into the dish.

11. Spoon the pesto over the pasta . . .

12. And sprinkle the Parmesan on top.

13. Toss until the pasta is coated in sauce. Let sit for 5 minutes, then give it one last stir.

14. Spoon servings into bowls . . .

15. And sprinkle on the toasted pine nuts!

VARIATIONS

- *Add 3 diced Roma tomatoes with the pasta and pesto.*
- *Add chunks of red bell pepper with the broccoli and cauliflower.*
- *Chop jarred roasted red peppers and stir them in when you add the pasta and pesto.*
- *Add diced pancetta to the vegetables before they go in the oven.*

The sauce is made in the oven!

MUSHROOM AND BLACK PEPPER PASTA

🕐 20 MINUTES **MAKES 4 TO 6 SERVINGS**

Mushroom lovers, it's time to perk up your ears and pay attention! (I'm speaking to myself as well, as a proud member of the Lifelong Mushroom Lovers' Union #471. They are everything to me.) This speedy pasta dish is creamy and simple, with a strong black pepper kick and a huge pile of mushrooms. The whole thing is such a total treat to eat. I wish I had a bowlful right now!

Kosher salt

8 ounces linguine

3 tablespoons butter

4 ounces cremini mushrooms, thinly sliced

4 ounces portobello mushrooms, thinly sliced

4 ounces white mushrooms, thinly sliced

3 garlic cloves, thinly sliced

1 shallot, diced

1 tablespoon cracked black pepper

¾ cup heavy cream

¼ cup grated Parmesan cheese, plus more for serving

Minced fresh flat-leaf parsley, for serving

1. Bring a pot of lightly salted water to a boil and add the linguine. Cook it for 2 minutes less than the package directions.

3. Melt the butter in a large skillet over medium heat. Add the mushrooms, garlic, and shallot . . .

5. Add a pinch of salt and the black pepper (don't worry if it looks like a lot—it is!) . . .

2. Using a glass measuring cup or heatproof pitcher, scoop out 1½ cups of the pasta water, then drain the pasta and set aside.

4. And cook, stirring frequently, until the liquid cooks off and the mushrooms are golden, 7 to 8 minutes.

6. And stir and cook for another couple of minutes.

A mushroom lover's dream!

7. Pour in the cream . . .

8. Then stir and let the cream boil gently and thicken, about 2 minutes.

9. Reduce the heat to low and add the Parmesan and drained pasta.

10. Use tongs to toss the pasta for a minute or two, coating it in the sauce. Pour in some of the reserved pasta water if the sauce gets too thick.

11. Dish up the pasta with plenty of the mushrooms . . .

12. And sprinkle on more Parmesan and some parsley.

~~~~~~~~~~~~~~~~~~~~~~

VARIATIONS

- *Grind tricolor peppercorns for little flecks of color.*
- *Add red pepper flakes for another level of heat.*
- *Substitute white wine for ¼ cup of the cream.*
- *Serve with sliced grilled chicken on top.*

Sister adventures with Betsy.

BAKED GOAT CHEESE PASTA

⏱ 35 MINUTES **MAKES 6 SERVINGS**

This is a version of the social media recipe that started the whole viral oven pasta sauce trend a few years ago. In the original, a block of feta is used, but I have found that goat cheese bakes and melts a lot more creamy and luscious! (Was that sentence grammatically sound? I thinketh not. Creamily and lusciously? Words are hard sometimes.)

This pasta is tomato-basil paradise, so I'll stop worrying about my words and just tell ya how to make it!

2 pints grape tomatoes

1 shallot, sliced

3 garlic cloves, sliced

3 tablespoons olive oil

2 tablespoons fresh oregano leaves

Kosher salt and ground black pepper

Pinch of red pepper flakes

One 8-ounce log goat cheese

8 ounces campanelle (or farfalle or other similar short pasta)

2 tablespoons prepared pesto

8 fresh basil leaves, cut into chiffonade

1. Preheat the oven to 425°F.

2. Place the tomatoes in a 9 × 13-inch baking dish . . .

4. And the olive oil, oregano leaves, a pinch of salt and black pepper, and the pepper flakes.

6. Then nestle the log of goat cheese in the center. Roast until the tomatoes have blistered and the goat cheese has softened, about 25 minutes.

3. Then add the shallot and garlic . . .

5. Toss until everything is mixed . . .

7. Bring a pot of lightly salted water to a boil, and when the tomatoes have about 10 minutes left, add the pasta to cook. Drain it when it's al dente, reserving the pasta water.

8. Remove the dish from the oven . . .

10. Add the pesto . . .

12. And gently stir everything together until the tomatoes start to break apart and the pasta is coated in the creamy sauce. Add a little more pasta water if needed for consistency. Sprinkle on the basil before serving!

9. Then pour in the pasta while it's still hot!

11. Drizzle in about ⅓ cup of the hot pasta water . . .

Todd's the youngest *and* tallest Drummond sib!

Cheers to oven pastas!

ONE-PAN PASTA ALLA NORMA

🕐 30 MINUTES **MAKES 6 SERVINGS**

I was, strangely, a very picky eater as a child. I say "strangely" because there's pretty much nothing I won't eat now—the only exception being bananas, which are still on my list of foods that will never, ever, not in a million years enter my mouth. However, during my childhood picky eating stage—which involved eating potato chip sandwiches and pepperoni pizza with the pepperoni removed after baking (I apologize for anyone who ever asked for my pizza order)—I did like a small handful of foods that defied understanding. Mushrooms were one; I still love them (see page 102). Spam was another; my dad is responsible. But possibly the weirdest one was eggplant. I think I had eggplant Parmesan in a restaurant somewhere, sometime, that must have been life-alteringly delicious. I still love eggplant today! (Spam . . . not so much.)

This is a one-pan version of a classic eggplant pasta dish, and the crispy breadcrumb topping is not to be skipped (or skimped on)! The crunch combines with the tender pasta and eggplant to create a true-love-forever situation. I adore, adore, adore this recipe!

2 tablespoons butter

1 cup seasoned panko breadcrumbs

2 tablespoons olive oil

1 medium eggplant, cut into medium dice

1 small yellow onion, halved and sliced

2 garlic cloves, thinly sliced

Kosher salt and ground black pepper

½ teaspoon red pepper flakes

Two 14.5-ounce cans stewed tomatoes

2½ cups low-sodium chicken broth, plus more as needed

12 ounces uncooked casarecce (or penne or farfalle)

1 cup freshly grated Parmesan cheese

½ cup mozzarella pearls or cubed fresh mozzarella

8 to 10 fresh basil leaves, cut into chiffonade, plus more leaves for serving

1. Melt the butter in a large deep skillet or Dutch oven over medium heat. Sprinkle in the panko . . .

2. And toast it, stirring constantly, until deep golden brown, about 3 minutes.

3. Remove it from the pan and set aside for serving.

4. Without cleaning the pan, heat the olive oil over medium heat and add the eggplant, onion, and garlic.

5. Sprinkle with salt and pepper, then cook, stirring frequently, until the eggplant and onion start to soften, about 3 minutes.

6. Add the pepper flakes and tomatoes . . .

Another one-pan winner of a pasta dinner!

7. The chicken broth . . .

8. And the pasta!

9. Stir until everything is combined . . .

10. Then cover the pot, reduce the heat to low, and cook, stirring occasionally . . .

11. Until the pasta is perfectly al dente, 12 to 14 minutes. If the liquid disappears before the pasta is fully cooked, splash in more broth as needed.

12. Turn off the heat and add the Parmesan . . .

13. And the mozzarella!

14. Stir just three or four times, until the cheeses are mixed in, but stop before the mozzarella is melted.

15. Stir in lots of fresh basil . . .

16. Then serve up big portions.

17. Sprinkle with a generous portion of crispy crumbs. Yum! Garnish each bowl with a couple basil leaves and serve.

~~~~~~~~~~

VARIATIONS

- *Substitute mushrooms for the eggplant.*
- *Substitute diced bell pepper for the eggplant.*
- *Add 2 tablespoons of pesto with the tomatoes.*
- *Add kalamata olives with the tomatoes.*

ITALIAN SAUSAGE PASTA SKILLET

🕐 25 MINUTES **MAKES 8 SERVINGS**

Looks-wise, this pasta-and-sausage skillet takes the cake. When I made it for this cookbook photo, I snapped a quick pic on my cell phone and posted it on social media. It received three billion likes! Not really three billion, but definitely at least a billion. If not a billion, then I know it had to be close to three thousand. Give or take. My point, and I have one, is that as gorgeous and appealing as this skillet dinner is, just wait until you enjoy a bowl of it. The pasta, the rustic chunks of sausage, the tender-crisp broccolini, the little piles of lemony ricotta . . . I mean, gosh!! It really is the cat's meow.

Kosher salt

1 pound farfalle

2 tablespoons olive oil

1 pound bulk Italian sausage

1 cup whole-milk ricotta cheese

Grated zest and juice of 1 lemon

Ground black pepper

1 yellow onion, halved and sliced

4 garlic cloves, minced

1 tablespoon fresh oregano leaves

1 bunch broccolini, cut into 1-inch pieces

½ cup jarred sliced roasted red peppers, drained

½ cup yellow cherry tomatoes, halved

½ cup freshly grated Parmesan cheese

2 teaspoons red pepper flakes

10 to 12 fresh basil leaves

1. Bring a large pot of lightly salted water to a boil and cook the pasta to al dente. Reserve about 2 cups of the pasta water, then drain the pasta and set aside.

2. Meanwhile, heat the olive oil in a large heavy skillet over medium-high heat and add the sausage, tearing it into chunks as you place it in the pan. Let it cook for 90 seconds without disturbing . . .

3. Then stir the sausage around to start cooking it on all sides.

4. Take a moment to whip up the ricotta mixture: In a small bowl, combine the ricotta, lemon zest, lemon juice, and a pinch of salt and pepper.

5. Stir until smooth and set aside.

6. Add the onion, garlic, and oregano to the pan with the sausage . . .

7. And cook, stirring the onion and sausage together until the sausage is cooked through, about 4 minutes.

8. Add the broccolini . . .

9. And the roasted red peppers . . .

10. And stir to mix everything together. Cook, stirring occasionally, for 5 minutes to give the broccolini a chance to become tender.

11. Drain the pasta and add it to the skillet . . .

12. Along with the tomatoes, Parmesan, and pepper flakes.

13. Stir to mix everything together, then turn off the heat. Add 1 cup of the reserved pasta water and stir for 1 minute to let the light sauce coat the veggies and pasta. Taste and add more salt and pepper if needed.

14. Dot with dollops of ricotta, then sprinkle the top with basil leaves. Scoop into bowls and serve, making sure everyone gets a ricotta dollop.

A totally gorgeous
pasta skillet!

GARLIC-LEMON SHRIMP PASTA

🕐 20 MINUTES **MAKES 6 SERVINGS**

Words almost fail me when I try to describe the delightful tastiness of this recipe. It's a little bit of a cross between shrimp scampi and shrimp Alfredo, but even that is an inadequate description! It's just simple, creamy, garlicky, shrimpy goodness . . . with plenty of pasta thrown in. And by the way, when I say "garlicky," I'm not joking around. There's a lot of it, and green onion, too . . . and your taste buds are gonna be doing backflips starting with the first bite. Wowzers!

Kosher salt

12 ounces penne

6 tablespoons butter

1½ pounds jumbo shrimp, peeled and deveined

8 garlic cloves, minced

5 green onions, sliced

½ cup jarred sliced roasted red peppers, drained

Grated zest and juice of 1 lemon

1 cup heavy cream

1 teaspoon red pepper flakes

Ground black pepper

¾ cup grated Parmesan cheese, plus more for serving

Fresh oregano leaves or basil leaves, for garnish

1. Bring a large pot of salted water to a boil and cook the pasta to al dente.

3. And the (excessive amount of!) garlic and green onions.

5. Add the roasted red pepper strips and stir them in . . .

2. Meanwhile, heat the oil and butter in a large skillet over medium-high heat, then add the shrimp . . .

4. Cook the shrimp until they're mostly pink but still slightly translucent, 1½ to 2 minutes, stirring often.

6. Then add the lemon zest and juice . . .

You'll love this creamy, lemony sauce!

7. And the luscious, heavenly cream!

10. When the pasta is done, drain it and add it to the pan . . .

12. Dish it into a bowl . . .

8. Stir, then add the red pepper flakes, salt, and pepper. Let the cream simmer and thicken, about 3 minutes.

11. Then stir until the pasta is coated in the cream sauce.

13. Then sprinkle with Parmesan and garnish with a few oregano or basil leaves.

9. Add the Parmesan and stir, then turn off the heat.

VARIATIONS

- *Substitute white wine for ¼ cup of the cream.*
- *Stir in diced fresh tomatoes right before serving.*
- *Make a super-indulgent version by swapping in raw lobster tail and scallops for some of the shrimp.*

Ladd, Ladd on the range . . .

ONE-PAN CAJUN CHICKEN ALFREDO

 35 MINUTES **MAKES 8 SERVINGS**

Glory, glory hallelujah! That's exactly what my silly food-loving soul wants to sing every time I make this incredible one-pan pasta dish, which encompasses everything my kids and I love. Cajun chicken and veggies are the star, but the creamy sauce is absolute heaven. It's got the spice, it's got the cheese, it's got the tender chicken (I mean, how good are chicken thighs?!?), and of course . . . it's got the noodles. And to top off all of these fantastic factors, it's all made in one pan! I'm madly in love.

6 boneless, skinless chicken thighs

3 tablespoons Cajun seasoning

Kosher salt and ground black pepper

1 tablespoon olive oil

1 tablespoon butter

1 medium onion, diced

2 bell peppers (any color), diced

4 garlic cloves, minced

1 tablespoon fresh oregano leaves

⅓ cup dry white wine

2½ cups low-sodium chicken broth, plus more as needed

1¼ cups heavy cream

10 ounces uncooked fusilli (or other short pasta)

1 tablespoon hot sauce, plus more to taste

1½ cups grated Parmesan cheese, plus more for serving

3 tablespoons minced fresh flat-leaf parsley, plus more for serving

1. Lay out the chicken thighs on a sheet pan or plate and season both sides with 1½ tablespoons of the Cajun seasoning. (If your Cajun seasoning does not contain any salt, sprinkle each piece of chicken with a pinch of salt and pepper.)

3. Remove the chicken to a plate and let it rest.

5. And stir and cook the vegetables until they start to soften, about 4 minutes.

2. Heat the oil and butter in a large skillet, then add the chicken and cook until browned on both sides and cooked through, about 4 minutes per side.

4. Add the onion, bell peppers, garlic, oregano, the remaining 1½ tablespoons Cajun seasoning, and a pinch of salt and pepper . . .

6. Pour in the wine . . .

The Drummond kids
inhale this pasta!

7. Then cook for 2 minutes, scraping the bottom of the pan to deglaze it.

8. Add the chicken broth . . .

9. And the cream. Stir to heat it up, then reduce the heat to low.

10. Add the pasta . . .

11. And stir it all together.

12. Cover the pan and cook, stirring three or four times, until the pasta is al dente, about 12 minutes. Splash in more broth if more liquid is needed to finish cooking the pasta.

13. Uncover the pan and stir the pasta, then add the juices from the plate of chicken and stir them in. Turn off the heat.

14. Slice the chicken thighs into strips.

15. Add the Parmesan and parsley to the pasta and stir to combine. Taste and adjust the seasonings if needed.

16. Serve up bowls of the pasta . . .

17. Lay chicken pieces on top . . .

18. And sprinkle on more Parmesan and parsley!

~~~~~~~~~~

VARIATIONS

- *Use 3 boneless, skinless chicken breasts instead of the thighs.*
- *Omit the chicken for a meatless meal.*
- *Swap in sliced mushrooms for some of the bell peppers.*
- *Add diced jalapeños or serrano peppers with the bell peppers to up the spice!*
- *Stir in 4 ounces of softened goat cheese with the Parmesan.*
- *Cut the chicken into bite-size pieces and stir them into the pasta just before serving.*

ONE-PAN SLOPPY JOE MAC

🕐 30 MINUTES **MAKES 8 SERVINGS**

I love coming up with homemade versions of Hamburger Helper. It makes me feel like a 1950s domestic goddess! Not that 1950s domestic goddesses made Hamburger Helper, considering it wasn't even invented until 1971. But they most certainly made dishes similar to this one, and that is what probably inspired the makers of Hamburger Helper to begin with! Isn't this whole thing incredibly ironic? Hamburger Helper was invented to help housewives make quicker versions of their everyday ground beef–based dinners, and here I am advocating for backward progress by encouraging you to make it from scratch again!

I'm a troublemaker, is what I am. But you are gonna love this one-pan recipe, which is a celebration of all the flavors of sloppy joes. The most delicious kind of trouble, if you ask me!

2 tablespoons olive oil

1 pound ground beef

1 small yellow onion, diced

3 garlic cloves, minced

1 green bell pepper, diced

2 teaspoons chili powder

Kosher salt and ground black pepper

12 ounces uncooked elbow macaroni

⅔ cup ketchup

1 tablespoon packed brown sugar

1 tablespoon Dijon mustard

3½ cups low-sodium beef broth

2½ cups grated mild cheddar cheese, plus more for garnish

Minced fresh flat-leaf parsley, for garnish

1. Heat the olive oil in a large skillet over medium-high heat. Add the ground beef, onion, and garlic . . .

2. Along with the green bell pepper, the chili powder, and a pinch of salt and pepper.

3. Cook, crumbling the beef . . .

4. Until it's cooked through, 7 to 8 minutes.

5. Add the macaroni . . .

6. The ketchup, brown sugar, and mustard . . .

Homemade Hamburger Helper!

7. And the broth.

10. When the macaroni is al dente and about three-quarters of the liquid has been absorbed, turn off the heat.

13. Serve up heapin' helpins . . .

8. Stir to combine . . .

11. Add the cheddar . . .

14. With a sprinkle of cheddar and parsley!

9. Then reduce the heat to low, cover the pan, and cook for 10 to 12 minutes, stirring two to three times during the cooking process.

12. And stir until it's totally melted in.

VARIATIONS

- *Add 8 ounces of sliced mushrooms along with the onions and peppers.*
- *Make a taco mac version by adding taco seasoning and pepper Jack cheese.*
- *Spice it up by adding red pepper flakes and hot sauce!*

PASTA FAGIOLI

45 MINUTES **MAKES 8 TO 10 SERVINGS**

This is a very, very classic Italian dish that translates to . . . are you ready? . . . pasta and beans! And oh, is it ever delicious. It's not really a soup, not strictly a pasta dish, and so much more than a stew. It's a down-right dandy bowlful of comforting deliciousness, and if you serve it with a loaf of warm crusty bread, even better! When I was young, I wanted so badly to be Italian. Long story. But my point is, I never feel closer to that childhood goal than when I whip up this recipe. You will inhale it!

¼ cup olive oil

1 yellow onion, diced

2 carrots, peeled and diced

3 celery stalks, thinly sliced

3 tablespoons fresh oregano leaves

1 tablespoon fresh thyme leaves

¼ teaspoon red pepper flakes

Kosher salt and ground black pepper

¼ cup tomato paste

6 garlic cloves, minced

6 cups low-sodium chicken broth

One 15-ounce can diced fire-roasted tomatoes

Two 15-ounce cans white beans (cannellini or Great Northern), drained and rinsed

1½ cups uncooked ditalini

3 cups roughly chopped kale (stems removed)

Grated zest and juice of 1 lemon

2 Roma tomatoes, seeded and diced

Grated Parmesan cheese, for serving

1. Heat the olive oil in a large Dutch oven over medium heat. Add the onion, carrots, celery, oregano, thyme, and pepper flakes.

3. And cook, stirring occasionally, until the vegetables have softened, about 7 minutes.

5. And cook for another 2 minutes, stirring constantly.

2. Add a pinch of salt and black pepper . . .

4. Add the tomato paste and garlic . . .

6. Pour in the chicken broth . . .

7. And the canned tomatoes.

8. And stir to combine. Increase the heat to medium-high and bring the mixture to a boil.

9. Place half the beans in a medium bowl and mash them with a fork until they're mostly broken up into smaller pieces and have formed a paste.

10. Add the mashed beans to the pot . . .

11. Along with the whole beans . . .

12. And the pasta.

13. Simmer, stirring often to keep the pasta from sticking together, until the flavors are developed, 10 to 12 minutes.

14. Pile in the kale (don't worry, it'll shrink!) . . .

15. And stir it in. Cook until the pasta is tender and the kale is wilted, another 5 minutes.

16. Add the lemon zest and juice . . .

17. And the Roma tomatoes. Stir and taste, adjusting the salt and pepper as needed.

18. Dish it up and sprinkle on Parmesan cheese!

That's amore!
(If ya know, ya know.)

PASTA WITH RUSTIC OVEN MEATBALLS

 45 MINUTES **MAKES 15 MEATBALLS, TO SERVE 4 TO 6**

If you happen to be in the mood for yet another oven-pasta triumph, this miraculous meaty marvel is about to make your month! It's got a few pretty clever elements, from an herb mixture that straddles the two main components to the timing of the meatballs and sauce . . . and you are going to feel energized by how relatively easy this spaghetti-and-meatballs-esque dish can actually be!

1 cup fresh flat-leaf parsley leaves, plus more for garnish

½ cup fresh basil leaves

¼ cup fresh oregano leaves

2 garlic cloves, minced

Grated zest and juice of ½ lemon

¼ cup olive oil

½ cup grated Parmesan cheese, plus more for serving

2 pints grape tomatoes

Kosher salt and ground black pepper

2 pounds ground beef

1 large egg

12 ounces bucatini

1. Position racks in the top and middle positions of the oven and preheat the oven to 425°F.

2. Add the parsley, basil, oregano, garlic, lemon zest, and lemon juice to a food processor (this is a mini one!) or blender.

3. Pulse the mixture several times to start pulverizing . . .

4. Then continue pulsing while adding the olive oil in a steady stream until the herbs form a paste.

5. Add the Parmesan . . .

6. And pulse to combine.

The meatballs and sauce
are cooked in the oven!

7. Place the tomatoes in a 9 × 13-inch baking dish and add half the herb mixture . . .

8. Then sprinkle with some salt and pepper . . .

9. And toss to coat the tomatoes. Set the baking dish aside.

10. Combine the ground beef and egg in a large bowl . . .

11. And add the rest of the herb paste and a pinch of salt and pepper.

12. Mix it with your hands until well combined . . .

13. Then pinch off rough balls of the mixture (1½ to 2 inches) and place them on a sheet pan. Place both the meatballs and the tomatoes in the oven (meatballs on the top rack, tomatoes on the middle rack) and roast everything until the meatballs are cooked through and the tomatoes are bursting open, 15 to 16 minutes.

14. While the meatballs and tomatoes are in the oven, bring a large pot of lightly salted water to a boil over high heat. Add the pasta and cook to al dente.

15. When the meatballs and tomatoes are done, remove them from the oven.

16. Drain the pasta, reserving a couple of cups of the pasta water, and pour it into the tomato dish.

17. Toss the pasta with the tomatoes, adding pasta water to form a light sauce. Make sure the noodles are fully coated in the sauce.

18. To serve, place the pasta with tomato sauce in a bowl and set a few meatballs on top.

19. Sprinkle with Parmesan and garnish with parsley.

VARIATIONS

- *Use 1 cup prepared pesto instead of the herb mixture to save time.*
- *Substitute Italian sausage for some of the ground beef.*
- *Use rigatoni instead of bucatini.*

Should I give them a lift?

Tex-Mex Family Favorites

I'm often asked to name my favorite category of food, and that's a tough one because, as is the case when attempting to name my favorite child, it changes day to day depending on the circumstances. But at any given moment, my answer would most frequently be Mexican food. The flavors, the heat, the color . . . there's just something about it that brings me back again and again and again, and endless variety opens a whole world of dinnertime possibilities.

I leave authentic Mexican food in the hands of those chefs and home cooks who know each dish's history and origins, and generally stick to the hybrid that has come to be known as Tex-Mex. These zesty dishes draw inspiration from Texas, Mexico, and even New Mexico, and all of them are perfect for lunch, dinner . . . or snacking with margaritas!

EASY TEX-MEX CHICKEN AND RICE

 25 MINUTES **MAKES 6 TO 8 SERVINGS**

I have always loved a saucy, zesty side of Mexican rice, and I have a recipe I've used for years that's hard to beat. So one dark and stormy night on the ranch (actually, I think it was a bright and sunny afternoon, but I like to be a drama queen sometimes), I added chicken to the mix and turned it into a main-dish casserole that I've been obsessed with ever since! It's so good with a green salad (and a margarita, but that's another story for another dark and stormy night), and using ready-to-go rice makes it a total keeper in my world!

1 tablespoon olive oil

2 pounds boneless, skinless chicken breasts, cut into bite-size pieces

1 teaspoon chili powder

1 teaspoon ground cumin

½ teaspoon cayenne pepper

¼ teaspoon ground turmeric

Kosher salt and ground black pepper

1 small yellow onion, diced

3 garlic cloves, minced

One 15-ounce can tomato sauce

One 10-ounce can Ro*tel (diced tomatoes and green chiles)

One 8.8-ounce bag microwavable white rice

1½ cups grated pepper Jack cheese

¼ cup crumbled queso fresco, for serving

Fresh cilantro leaves, for serving

1. In a high-sided skillet over medium-high heat, heat the olive oil. Add the chicken, chili powder, cumin, cayenne, turmeric, and a pinch of salt and pepper.

2. Stir the chicken to coat it in the spices, then add the onion and garlic and cook, stirring constantly, until the onion is starting to soften and the chicken is halfway cooked, about 3 minutes.

3. Pour in the tomato sauce and Ro*tel . . .

So delicious with a salad!

4. And the rice. (No need to heat it up beforehand!)

6. Reduce the heat to low and sprinkle the pepper Jack all over the surface.

8. Turn off the heat and sprinkle on the queso fresco . . .

5. Stir together and cook until the sauce is bubbly, the chicken is cooked, and the rice is heated through, about 5 minutes. Taste and adjust the seasonings if needed.

7. Put the lid on the pan and let the mixture simmer until the cheese is melted completely, about 3 minutes.

9. And garnish with the cilantro.

VARIATION

- *Use a mix of chicken breasts and chicken thighs for both light and dark meat.*

Burning with Betsy and the cowboys.

PINEAPPLE CHICKEN TACOS

 25 MINUTES **MAKES 4 SERVINGS**

There is *sooooo* much going on in these tasty tacos that it's almost hard for me to describe it all in a single paragraph, let alone a single sentence . . . but I'll try. Tender, seasoned chicken thighs pan-cooked and simmered in a pineapple sauce, then sliced and piled in tacos with a creamy, chipotle broccoli slaw and topped with fresh pineapple and pickled peppers. Whew! I'm out of breath! And that was the cold, factual version. When you make them yourself and take a bite, it'll all come to life in a wonderful way. These tacos are rockin' my taco life!

2 tablespoons olive oil

6 boneless, skinless chicken thighs

Kosher salt and ground black pepper

12 ounces store-bought broccoli slaw

½ cup Honey Chipotle Crema (page 24), plus more for serving (or sour cream or ranch dressing)

¼ cup fresh cilantro leaves, plus more for serving

2 garlic cloves, minced

4 green onions, sliced

One 6-ounce can pineapple juice

2 tablespoons honey

2 tablespoons hot sauce

Small (street taco– or fajita-size) flour or corn tortillas, warmed, for serving

½ cup thinly sliced pineapple wedges, for serving

Pickled Peppers (page 4) or jarred jalapeños, for serving

1. Heat the oil in a large skillet over medium-high heat. Season the chicken on both sides with salt and pepper and add it to the pan. Let it cook undisturbed for about 2 minutes.

3. And stir to coat the slaw in the dressing. Taste and add more salt and pepper as needed.

2. Meanwhile, make the slaw: Combine the broccoli slaw and chipotle crema in a large bowl. Sprinkle in a pinch of salt and pepper . . .

4. Add the cilantro leaves and stir them in, then set the slaw aside to develop the flavors a bit. (You can make this up to a couple of hours ahead of time and keep it in the fridge!)

5. Back to the chicken! Turn the pieces over and add the garlic and green onions . . .

6. Then stir and move the chicken around the pan for another minute or so.

7. Reduce the heat to medium-low, then pour in the pineapple juice.

8. Squeeze in the honey . . .

9. Shake in the hot sauce . . .

10. And stir the chicken around the pan as the sauce mixes. Let the chicken simmer until it's cooked through, another 5 minutes.

11. Remove the chicken to a cutting board, reduce the heat to low, and whisk the pan sauce, scraping the bottom of the pan to loosen up any small bits. Splash in a little hot water if the skillet is too dry. Turn off the heat.

12. Slice the chicken . . .

13. Then return it to the skillet. Toss to coat it in the sauce.

14. Build tacos by placing a small amount of chicken on a tortilla . . .

15. Then topping with slaw, pineapple chunks, pickled peppers, and chipotle crema. Add hot sauce and cilantro!

Page 24!

My favorite tacos
these days!

SANTA FE EGGS IN PURGATORY

⏱ 35 MINUTES **MAKES 4 TO 6 SERVINGS**

Shakshuka is a classic (and very popular in recent years) North African dish that involves baking eggs in a flavorful, spicy tomato sauce until they're perfectly poached. There's a similar Italian version called Eggs in Purgatory, which both delights and cracks me up. Purgatory must be a delicious (albeit hot and fiery) place!

In a Tex-Mex play on the originals, this brings in a chunky homemade salsa verde rather than the traditional red sauce. It's absolutely to die for! (That is not meant to be a purgatory reference, by the way.)

1 large yellow onion, cut into wedges

4 tomatillos, husks removed

2 poblano chiles, stems removed and halved

2 jalapeños, stems removed

5 garlic cloves, peeled

3 tablespoons olive oil

½ teaspoon ground cumin

½ teaspoon dried oregano

Kosher salt and ground black pepper

½ cup fresh cilantro leaves

Grated zest and juice of 1 lime

6 large eggs

FOR SERVING

Small (street taco– or fajita-size) flour tortillas

Sliced avocado

Sour cream

Hot sauce

1. Preheat the broiler.

2. Place the onion wedges, tomatillos, poblanos, jalapeños, and garlic cloves on a sheet pan. Drizzle on the olive oil . . .

3. And add the cumin, oregano, and a pinch of salt and pepper.

4. Toss to coat the veggies in the oil and seasonings . . .

5. Then broil them on the top rack of the oven for 5 minutes, or until charred on the surface. Adjust the oven temperature to 400°F.

6. Transfer the veggies to a food processor or blender . . .

7. Along with the oil and the blackened bits from the sheet pan.

Eggs baked in green chile sauce. Yum!

8. Add the cilantro, lime zest, and lime juice, then put the lid on the blender and pulse a few times . . .

9. Until you have a nice chunky salsa verde!

10. Pour the salsa verde into a 3-quart baking dish and spread it into an even layer.

11. Use the handle of a wooden spoon to make six wells in the salsa . . .

12. And carefully crack an egg into each well. Sprinkle each egg with a little salt and pepper . . .

13. Then bake until the whites are mostly opaque but the yolks are still somewhat soft, about 12 minutes.

14. Meanwhile, char the tortillas over an open flame, holding them with metal tongs. (Alternatively, you can warm them in the microwave for 30 seconds!)

15. Carefully scoop out each egg, making sure to get plenty of the salsa along with it.

16. Serve it with a tortilla, avocado, sour cream, and hot sauce.

Jalapeño Popper Quesadillas

🕐 30 MINUTES MAKES 2 QUESADILLAS, TO SERVE 2 TO 4

I love anything that celebrates jalapeño poppers, the cream cheese–stuffed, bacon-wrapped jalapeño appetizer our family has loved for years and years. I've seen jalapeño popper burgers, pizza, and grilled cheese, and it was only a matter of time before a jalapeño popper quesadilla burst onto the scene. It's a treat and a half!

4 slices bacon

4 ounces (half a package) cream cheese, softened

⅔ cup grated pepper Jack cheese

1 teaspoon cayenne pepper

½ teaspoon ground cumin

4 burrito-size tortillas

2 jalapeños, seeded and cut into long thin slices

2 tablespoons butter

Big Al's Pico Tomorrow (page 21), for serving

1. In a large skillet over medium heat, cook the bacon until crisp, about 8 minutes.

3. In a medium bowl, combine the cream cheese, pepper Jack, cayenne, and cumin.

5. Spread half of the mixture on one of the tortillas, leaving a ½-inch border around the edges.

2. Remove the bacon to a paper towel–lined plate, turn off the heat, and pour off the excess grease (or dab it with paper towels). You want the flavor but not all the fat!

4. Stir and smush the mixture together until it's well combined.

6. Add half the jalapeño slices all over the cream cheese and tear 2 slices of the bacon into pieces, sprinkling it all over.

*Big Al's Pico Tomorrow
(page 21)!*

**Jalapeños, cream
cheese, and bacon??
Sign me up!**

7. Turn the heat under the skillet to medium-low and add 1 tablespoon of the butter. When it's melted, lay the tortilla with cream cheese in the pan and place a second tortilla on top.

8. Cook the quesadilla on the first side, watching constantly to make sure it doesn't burn, about 4 minutes. Flip it over when the surface is golden and the filling is starting to soften and melt.

9. Cook it on the second side for an additional 3 minutes or so, until the filling is totally soft and gooey. Use a pizza cutter or knife to cut it into 6 wedges and serve immediately. (Make the second quesadilla with the rest of the ingredients.) Serve with pico de gallo!

VARIATIONS

- *Add shredded cooked chicken to the quesadilla.*
- *Add a 4-ounce can of diced green chiles to the cheese mixture.*
- *Serve with BBQ sauce for dipping.*

Ladd + Shorts = "Lorts"

Big Al's Pico Tomorrow (page 21)!

Veggies and cheese everywhere you turn!

ROASTED VEGETABLE QUESADILLAS

⏱ 40 MINUTES MAKES 3 QUESADILLAS, TO SERVE 3 OR 4

I'm not sure how many quesadilla recipes I have shared on my website, my cooking show, and in my cookbooks since I first started blogging in 2006, but my guess would be somewhere around 9,000. I know that isn't technically possible considering I only started blogging around 5,205 days ago, and even though quesadillas are my favorite food on earth, I don't think that amount of cheese has ever existed. Or has it? I'll have to ponder that one.

Point is, there is no limit to my love for quesadillas, and the variations are absolutely endless. But of all the options I've fiddled and experimented with through the years, this version we've served at The Mercantile is top three for sure! Flavorful veggies, creamy cheese—yes, please!

1 cup sour cream

¼ cup milk

Grated zest and juice of 1 lime

½ cup minced fresh cilantro

Kosher salt and ground black pepper

5 tablespoons butter

1 small yellow onion, halved and sliced (or 1 cup Caramelized Onions, page 12)

1 small zucchini, halved lengthwise and sliced

1 yellow bell pepper, cut into thin strips

1 red bell pepper, cut into thin strips

1 poblano chile, seeded and cut into thin strips

1 Anaheim chile, seeded and cut into thin strips

2 tablespoons olive oil

Three 10-inch spinach tortillas

3 cups grated Monterey Jack cheese

½ cup frozen roasted corn, thawed

Five-Minute Salsa (page 17), for serving

Big Al's Pico Tomorrow (page 21), for serving

1. First, make the cilantro-lime crema: Combine the sour cream, milk, lime zest, lime juice, cilantro, and a pinch of salt and pepper in a small bowl. Mix well and set aside.

2. Melt 2 tablespoons of the butter in a medium skillet over medium-low heat. Add the onion and sprinkle in a pinch of salt and pepper.

3. Cook the onion, stirring frequently . . .

4. Until they are caramelized and deep in color, about 8 minutes. Remove them from the skillet and set aside.

5. Preheat the broiler and lay the zucchini, both bell peppers, poblano chile, and Anaheim chile on a sheet pan. Drizzle with the olive oil, sprinkle with salt and pepper, and toss to coat.

6. Broil the veggies until the edges start to char, 5 to 6 minutes, taking care that they don't burn.

7. Over low heat, melt 1 tablespoon of the butter in the same skillet you used to cook the onions. Lay one tortilla in the pan.

8. Sprinkle one-third of the cheese all over the surface of the tortilla.

9. Place one-third of the onions on one side of the tortilla.

10. Top the onions with one-third of the roasted veggies, then sprinkle on about one-third of the corn.

11. Cook the quesadilla until the cheese is totally melted and the tortilla is golden underneath, taking care not to burn the tortilla.

12. Using a spatula, carefully flip the half with cheese over on top of the half with the veggies.

13. Remove it to a cutting board and slice it into 4 wedges. Make two more quesadillas just like this one. (You can use a larger griddle to make more than one at a time!) Serve with the cilantro-lime crema, the salsa, and the pico de gallo.

TEQUILA SHRIMP STREET TACOS

🕐 20 MINUTES **MAKES 4 SERVINGS**

I'm a huge fan of bang bang shrimp, a popular appetizer made famous by a restaurant called Bonefish Grill. I first had the shrimp at the location in Atlanta, and once I learned that mayonnaise was a primary contributor to the signature creamy sauce, the mysterious deliciousness all made sense. I decided one day to turn it into a soft taco situation, then over time turned the sauce more in a spicy Tex-Mex direction (with some Cajun flavors thrown in). The end result? Complete taco bliss. Prepare to be bowled over!

4 tablespoons (½ stick) butter

2 tablespoons olive oil

1 pound jumbo shrimp (16/20 per pound), peeled and deveined

4 garlic cloves, minced

2 green onions, sliced

1 jalapeño, thinly sliced

1 tablespoon Cajun seasoning

¼ cup tequila

⅓ cup mayonnaise

2 tablespoons hot sauce

FRESNO PEPPER SLAW

1 cup thinly shaved cabbage (a mix of white and red is good!)

½ cup minced fresh cilantro

1 Fresno pepper, sliced into thin rings

1 lime, halved

1 tablespoon honey

Kosher salt and ground black pepper

FOR SERVING

Small (street taco– or fajita-size) flour tortillas, blackened (see page 140)

Sliced avocado

Fresh cilantro

Pickled jalapeño slices

1. Melt the butter with the oil in a large skillet over medium-high heat. Add the shrimp in a single layer and cook for 2 minutes . . .

2. Then turn them over to the other side.

3. Add the garlic, green onions, and jalapeño . . .

4. And sprinkle in the Cajun seasoning.

5. Stir and finish cooking the shrimp for 2 minutes, coating it in the Cajun seasoning.

6. Turn off the heat, pour in the tequila . . .

The most scrumptious
shrimp you'll ever taste!

7. And stir as the tequila forms a bit of sauce.

8. In a small bowl, stir together the mayonnaise and the hot sauce.

9. Add the mayo mixture to the skillet . . .

10. And stir until the sauce is creamy and the shrimp are totally coated. Set aside.

11. Make the Fresno pepper slaw: In a large bowl, combine the cabbage, cilantro, and Fresno chile. Squeeze in the lime juice . . .

12. And the honey, then sprinkle in a pinch of salt and pepper . . .

13. And toss everything together for a couple of minutes to give the cabbage a chance to mix with the lime and honey.

14. Build a taco by putting some shrimp on one of the blackened tortillas . . .

15. Piling on some slaw . . .

16. And adding a couple of slices of avocado, more cilantro, and some slices of pickled jalapeño. Delicious!

VARIATIONS

- *Use plain Greek yogurt instead of mayonnaise (or sub it for half!) for a lighter dish.*
- *Serve the shrimp by itself as an appetizer!*
- *Substitute bite-size pieces of chicken breast for the shrimp.*

**Country dogs get up
before the sun rises!**

SPEEDY CHILI VERDE

⏱ 30 MINUTES **MAKES 6 TO 8 SERVINGS**

After having traveled to New Mexico a few times, I would like to report that when asked the difficult question of whether I prefer red or green chili, my answer is always the same: "Yes." Because the truth is, I can't decide. Both are perfect, and I could alternate for the rest of my life and never be able to pick a favorite. But when I'm craving the green, I've fallen in love with this lightning-fast version, which can be ready to dish up in thirty minutes if you play your cards right! I used to use ground beef for this, but subbed in breakfast sausage one evening in a pinch, and it has wound up being my go-to. I predict it'll be your go-to, too! (*Go-to, too* . . . that's fun to say.)

2 tablespoons olive oil

2 tablespoons butter

1 large yellow onion, diced

4 garlic cloves, minced

2 large poblano chiles, diced

1 jalapeño, seeded and finely diced

2 pounds spicy breakfast sausage (such as J.C. Potter or Jimmy Dean)

Two 15-ounce cans green enchilada sauce

One 16-ounce jar salsa verde

One 4-ounce can diced green chiles

1 lime, halved

Kosher salt and ground black pepper

FOR SERVING

Sour cream

Sliced radishes

Fresh cilantro leaves

Hot sauce

Lime wedges

1. Heat the olive oil and butter in a large Dutch oven over medium-high heat. Add the onion, garlic, poblanos, and jalapeño . . .

4. And cook until it's totally browned, crumbling the meat as you stir, about 8 minutes. Drain off most of the excess fat, leaving a little for flavor.

2. And cook for 3 minutes, stirring often, to start softening the vegetables.

5. Add the enchilada sauce . . .

3. Add the sausage meat . . .

6. The salsa verde . . .

Sausage gives
this chili amazing
flavor!

7. And the green chiles.

8. Stir everything together, bring it to a boil, reduce the heat, and simmer for 10 to 12 minutes, stirring occasionally.

9. Squeeze in the lime juice and stir it in, then taste and add salt and pepper if needed.

10. Dish it up and garnish with sour cream, radishes, cilantro leaves, and hot sauce. Serve with lime wedges on the side.

VARIATIONS

- Substitute ground beef for half the sausage, or do a full ground beef version.
- Do a red chili version by substituting red enchilada sauce and chipotle salsa. Substitute 4 chopped chipotle peppers for the green chiles.
- Garnish with grated pepper Jack cheese.

Bryce plays football at OSU. Go Bryce, and *go Pokes!*

BREAKFAST TORTILLA BAKE

⏱ 35 MINUTES **MAKES 4 SERVINGS**

This breakfast-for-dinner delight is a nifty cross between a casserole and a quesadilla . . . with eggs thrown in! Once you master the process of baking cheese, veggies, and eggs in a neat tortilla shell, your creativity (and taste buds!) will come alive, and you'll never put your 10-inch skillet back in the cabinet!

By the way, can we normalize eggs for dinner? Because they're totally not just for breakfast anymore.

1 tablespoon olive oil

1 medium yellow onion, halved and thinly sliced

1 green bell pepper, thinly sliced

4 ounces cremini or white button mushrooms, sliced

Kosher salt and ground black pepper

1 cup packed baby spinach

One 12-inch flour tortilla

1 cup grated Colby-Jack cheese

4 large eggs

2 green onions, thinly sliced

Hot sauce, for serving

1. Preheat the oven to 375°F.

2. Heat the olive oil in a 10-inch ovenproof skillet over medium-high heat. Add the onion, bell pepper, mushrooms, and a pinch of salt and pepper.

4. Turn off the heat and add the spinach, then stir until it's totally mixed in with the vegetables. (It will naturally wilt as you stir.)

6. Without cleaning the skillet, lay the tortilla in the skillet and press it onto the bottom of the pan, letting it cover the sides.

3. Cook the veggies, stirring frequently, until they are soft and starting to brown around the edges, 6 to 7 minutes.

5. Remove the vegetables to a plate.

7. Sprinkle in two-thirds of the cheese . . .

Everything's baked in a tortilla!

8. And add the vegetables to the top of the cheese. Spread them into an even layer.

11. Sprinkle each egg with salt and pepper . . .

14. Sprinkle the top with green onions and serve it right out of the skillet . . .

9. Use the handle of a wooden spoon to make four wells in the vegetables . . .

12. Then sprinkle the rest of the cheese around the eggs, avoiding the yolks.

15. Or use a spatula to slide it onto a cutting board and cut it into wedges. Serve with hot sauce!

VARIATIONS

- *Use any veggies you like: tricolor bell peppers, sliced zucchini, and so on.*
- *Use pepper Jack cheese instead of Colby-Jack.*

10. Then carefully crack an egg in each of the wells.

13. Bake until the cheese has melted and the whites of the eggs are opaque, 15 to 17 minutes.

Winner Winner Chicken Dinners

If beef is the star of the dinnertime show in my family, chicken is most definitely the workhorse. Where a thick, juicy steak is fine on its own, I think of chicken as more of a blank canvas on which to paint a masterpiece of flavor, texture, and color! There are so many different cuts—tenders, breasts, cutlets, thighs—not to mention the choice between light and dark meat . . . and boneless vs. bone-in! Considering all the possibilities, you may consider the list of chicken recipes below to be somewhat short. But that's because chicken appears in several other dishes throughout this cookbook! It's such a staple, it rears its awesome head everywhere.

(Well, except the steak chapter. That goes without saying.)

BBQ-GLAZED CHICKEN

⏱ 20 MINUTES   MAKES 8 PIECES GLAZED CHICKEN, TO SERVE 4 TO 8

I was afraid to call this dish "BBQ-Glazed Chicken" because I was afraid it would undersell what has become my very top choice for a chicken dinner on any given night. It has all the juiciness and flavor of barbecue chicken made outside in the summertime (from the blackened edges to the sticky sauce), but without the mosquitos . . . and without the chicken bones! It's tender and flavorful and oh-so-comforting, and I love it so much, it's on the menu at my restaurant! Don't let the ordinary ol' name fool ya. This dinner will surprise and delight you again and again and again!

Page 311

Page 293

Truly the tastiest barbecue chicken I've ever had!

1 tablespoon packed brown sugar

1 teaspoon chili powder

1 teaspoon paprika

1 teaspoon kosher salt

½ teaspoon garlic powder

½ teaspoon ground black pepper

4 chicken breast cutlets

4 boneless, skinless chicken thighs

2 tablespoons butter

2 tablespoons olive oil

1 cup barbecue sauce, plus more for serving

1 green onion, sliced

Instant Cheesy Mash (page 311), or any mashed potatoes, for serving

Balsamic Brussels Sprouts (page 293), for serving

1. In a small bowl, mix the brown sugar, chili powder, paprika, kosher salt, garlic powder, and black pepper.

4. Sprinkle the other half of the seasoning over the chicken.

7. Serve a chicken breast and thigh over mashed potatoes, or just one piece per serving for a smaller portion.

2. Lay the chicken pieces on a sheet pan or plate and sprinkle the tops with half the seasoning mix.

5. Cook the chicken for 5 minutes, moving it around the pan as it cooks, then flip it to the other side.

8. Sprinkle on some green onions. (And serve with your favorite veggie on the side!)

3. Heat the butter and olive oil in a very large cast-iron skillet over medium-high heat and add the chicken, seasoning side down. (You can cook it in two batches if you'd like to use a normal-size pan!)

6. Top each piece of chicken with about 2 tablespoons of barbecue sauce, then reduce the heat to low and cook until the chicken is done, an additional 3 to 4 minutes.

~~~~~~~~~~~~~~~~

VARIATIONS

- *Use boneless or bone-in pork chops instead of chicken.*
- *Make a barbecue chicken sandwich by putting one piece of the chicken on a small, standard hamburger bun.*
- *Dice the cooked chicken and add it to pizza for a terrific topping.*

CREAMY LEMON CHICKEN WITH NOODLES

 35 MINUTES **MAKES 3 TO 6 SERVINGS**

Lemon and chicken are natural bedfellows, and I'm always twisting my mustache and scheming on new evil ways to throw them together. I could eat this gloriously simple supper once a week for the rest of my life and never get tired of its lemony garlicky chickeny goodness! There's something about the egg noodles here; they catch all of the cream sauce in such a nice way. Dang, I love this dinner!

½ cup all-purpose flour

Kosher salt and ground black pepper

6 boneless, skinless chicken thighs

3 tablespoons olive oil

12 ounces egg noodles

4 garlic cloves, minced

⅓ cup dry white wine

¾ cup heavy cream

2 lemons, 1 juiced and zested and 1 cut into 6 thin slices

4 packed cups spinach

½ cup grated Parmesan cheese

4 tablespoons (½ stick) butter, melted

3 tablespoons minced fresh parsley

1. In a shallow pan or dish, combine the flour with a generous pinch of salt and pepper.

3. Heat the olive oil in a large pan over medium-high heat, then add the chicken . . .

5. Meanwhile, bring a pot of lightly salted water to a boil, then add the egg noodles to start the cooking.

2. Working with a couple of pieces at a time, season both sides of the chicken with salt and pepper, then dredge in the flour, shaking off the excess.

4. And cook it, gently moving it around the pan occasionally, until golden brown on both sides and cooked through, about 4 minutes per side. Remove the chicken to a sheet pan and turn off the heat.

6. While the noodles are cooking, turn the heat to medium, then add the garlic to the pan you cooked the chicken in. Stir it around to start to release the flavor, about 1 minute.

Such a light, lemony,
luscious meal!

7. While stirring the garlic, pour in the wine and scrape the bits off the bottom of the pan. Let the wine reduce for 1 minute.

8. Pour in the cream . . .

9. Along with the lemon juice and half the grated zest and a pinch of salt and pepper.

10. Stir and cook until the sauce has thickened, 2 to 3 minutes.

11. Reduce the heat to low and drop in the spinach . . .

12. And the Parmesan.

13. Stir as the spinach starts to wilt.

14. Return the chicken to the pan, nestling it into the sauce, and let it cook for 2 minutes to warm the chicken through.

15. Lay a lemon slice on each piece of chicken, then sprinkle on the remaining lemon zest. Turn off the heat.

16. Drain the pasta and pour it into a large bowl, then drizzle in the melted butter.

17. Add the parsley and a generous pinch of salt and pepper. Toss to combine.

18. Pile the noodles into wide bowls and top with the chicken and a drizzle of cream sauce.

VARIATIONS

- Use chicken breast cutlets instead of thighs.
- Add thinly sliced mushrooms to the pan with the garlic.
- Substitute spaghetti or linguine for the egg noodles.
- Stir 2 tablespoons of pesto into the cream sauce.

Ladd and
his summer crew!

CHICKEN POT PIE SKILLET

🕐 30 MINUTES **MAKES 6 SERVINGS**

Chicken pot pie is a comfort food classic, but it sure can take centuries to make from scratch. There's the filling, there's the pie crust . . . and then there's the baking the filling in the pie crust, which by itself can take upwards of two years! Yes, I am an exaggerator. Can't help it! It's from my years as a middle child.

So here's a solution! This skillet version shaves a thousand years off the whole process (give or take an hour or two), the end result is absolutely yummy, and I think you're going to be instantly smitten.

2 tablespoons butter

2 tablespoons olive oil

3 chicken breast cutlets

Kosher salt and ground black pepper

1 unbaked refrigerated pie crust (sold in a roll)

1 teaspoon fresh thyme leaves, plus more for garnish

½ cup plus 2 tablespoons heavy cream

1 yellow onion, diced

3 garlic cloves, minced

¼ cup all-purpose flour

2 cups low-sodium chicken broth

2 cups frozen vegetable medley

1. Preheat the oven to 425°F.

2. Heat the butter and oil in a large skillet over medium heat. Season the chicken on both sides with salt and pepper . . .

4. Meanwhile, unroll the pie crust onto a piece of parchment paper and sprinkle half of the thyme leaves over the top.

6. Brush 2 tablespoons of the cream all over the surface of the dough round.

3. And cook them until golden and cooked through, 3 to 4 minutes per side.

5. Run a rolling pin over the surface in order to press the leaves into the dough.

7. Lay the dough round on a sheet pan and bake until crisp and golden, 9 to 11 minutes. Set it aside.

A fast chicken
pot pie . . . finally!

8. Remove the chicken to a plate . . .

9. Then add the onion and garlic to the skillet . . .

10. And cook, stirring frequently, until the onion starts to soften, 4 to 5 minutes.

11. Sprinkle in the flour . . .

12. And cook, stirring, for 1 minute, until the onion is well coated and the flour is cooked a bit.

13. Pour in the broth, stirring as it incorporates. Let the mixture cook until thickened slightly, about 3 minutes.

14. Stir in the remaining ½ cup cream . . .

15. Then add a pinch of salt and pepper and the remaining ½ teaspoon thyme. Reduce the heat to low and let the sauce simmer and thicken further, about 5 minutes.

16. Transfer the chicken to a cutting board and cut it into bite-size pieces.

17. Add the vegetables to the sauce and stir them in . . .

18. Then stir in the chicken!

19. Let the mixture simmer for a few more minutes, tasting and adjusting the seasonings as needed.

20. Ladle helpings into individual bowls . . .

21. Then break off pieces of the crust . . .

22. And stick them in the bowls with the filling. Garnish with a sprinkle of thyme leaves.

~~~~~~~~~~~~~~~~~~

VARIATIONS

- *Add a pinch of turmeric to the chicken filling as it cooks to give it a golden tint.*
- *Substitute white wine or sherry for ⅓ cup of the broth for a yummy flavor.*
- *Use biscuit dough, puff pastry, or even pizza crust instead of pie crust.*

Camo cowboy!

CHICKEN SALTIMBOCCA

🕐 30 MINUTES **MAKES 4 SERVINGS**

Get ready, friends. *Just get ready.* This incomprehensibly stunning chicken dish is so easy to make, you'll actually feel guilty for pulling off something so sublime with so little effort! But it's the most delicious guilt you'll ever experience, if that's any consolation. I can't really describe how good this is in words, so I'll take that as my cue to stop talking now.

4 chicken breast cutlets

Kosher salt and ground black pepper

14 fresh sage leaves

4 pieces very thinly sliced prosciutto

2 tablespoons butter

2 tablespoons olive oil

4 slices mozzarella cheese

1 garlic clove, minced

1 cup low-sodium chicken broth

1 cup heavy cream

1. Preheat the oven to 375°F.

2. Season both sides of the chicken with a pinch of salt and pepper, then place them on a sheet pan and lay 2 sage leaves on each piece.

4. And tuck the ends underneath. You want the prosciutto to adhere to the chicken!

6. Cook the chicken for 4 to 5 minutes to crisp the prosciutto, then flip and cook 4 to 5 minutes more.

3. Lay a piece of prosciutto diagonally across each piece of chicken . . .

5. Heat 1 tablespoon of the butter and the olive oil in a large cast-iron skillet over medium heat. Add the wrapped chicken pieces, sage side down.

7. Remove the pieces of chicken to a sheet pan . . .

Crispy Parmesan Potatoes (page 290)!

A fantastic new favorite of mine!

8. Then top them with the mozzarella and place the pan in the oven for about 5 minutes to let the mozzarella melt.

9. Add the remaining 1 tablespoon butter to the skillet. Chop the remaining 6 sage leaves and add them to the skillet, along with the garlic.

10. Stir and cook for 1 minute to release the flavors . . .

11. Then add the broth . . .

12. And the cream. (Have I mentioned there's lots of cream in this sauce? Ha ha.)

13. Stir and cook for 3 minutes or so, until the sauce is bubbly and thick. Taste and season with salt and pepper.

14. Spoon some sauce onto a plate. (Psst. I'm serving the chicken with Crispy Parmesan Potatoes, page 290!)

15. Remove the chicken when the cheese is melted . . .

16. And place one of the pieces on top of the sauce. Top with more sauce if you'd like!

ITALIAN CHICKEN LETTUCE WRAPS

🕐 30 MINUTES **MAKES 6 TO 8 SERVINGS**

Setting a board of build-your-own snack options in front of friends or family always invites fun. Everyone serves themselves and is in charge of their own food destiny . . . at least for that meal! I love this simple chicken-and-fixins version of lettuce wraps. It has an Italian vibe, the whole thing comes together in about 30 minutes, and the presentation is memorably marvelous.

¼ cup plus 2 tablespoons olive oil

1 tablespoon minced fresh rosemary leaves

½ teaspoon red pepper flakes

3 garlic cloves, minced

Grated zest and juice of 1 lemon

1 teaspoon kosher salt, plus more as needed

½ teaspoon ground black pepper, plus more as needed

4 chicken breast cutlets

1 cup grape tomatoes, quartered

½ small red onion, diced small

FOR SERVING

½ cup grated Pecorino Romano cheese

½ cup crumbled feta cheese

¼ cup prepared pesto

¼ cup pine nuts, toasted (see steps 7 and 8 on page 100)

Fresh basil leaves

Balsamic glaze

10 to 12 butter lettuce leaves

1. In a large bowl, mix ¼ cup of the olive oil, the rosemary, pepper flakes, garlic, lemon zest, salt, and black pepper until well combined.

2. Add the chicken and toss it to coat.

3. Preheat a grill pan or cast-iron skillet to medium heat and cook both sides of the chicken until it's fully cooked and the surface has great grill marks, 4 to 5 minutes per side.

4. Remove the chicken to a cutting board to rest for a few minutes, then cut it into bite-size pieces.

5. To make the tomato topping, in a medium bowl, place the tomatoes, onion, remaining 2 tablespoons olive oil, the lemon juice, and a pinch of salt and pepper.

8. Then everyone can dive in and build away! Fill a piece of lettuce with all the elements, then grab it like a taco and devour!

~~~~~~~~~~~~~~~~

VARIATIONS

- *Add dishes of chopped artichoke hearts, mozzarella pearls, assorted olives, or roasted red pepper for more filling options.*

- *Save even more time by using pre-cooked chicken.*

6. Stir to combine.

7. Build a board with the chicken, tomato topping, Romano cheese, feta cheese, pesto, pine nuts, basil leaves, balsamic glaze, and lettuce leaves.

I still tag along with Ladd sometimes. (Emphasis on sometimes!)

A bountiful
build-your-own board!

MANGO CHICKEN

⏱ 40 MINUTES **MAKES 6 SERVINGS**

Mango salsa can readily be found at supermarkets these days, which is very, very, very good news considering how (a) easy, (b) good-looking, and (c) outlandishly yummy this skillet dinner is. One glance at the ingredients list below will tell the story of how simple it is, and it's also one of those marvels that's as perfect as a weeknight dinner as it is a supper for company! Turmeric is responsible for the deep golden color, which just adds to the appeal. You've gotta make this soon!

6 boneless, skinless chicken thighs

Kosher salt and ground black pepper

2 tablespoons olive oil

1 medium yellow onion, halved and thinly sliced

3 garlic cloves, minced

½ teaspoon ground turmeric, plus more as needed for color

1 cup long-grain white rice

One 16-ounce jar mango salsa, plus more for serving if desired

2 teaspoons chili powder

Fresh cilantro, for garnish

Lime wedges, for serving

1. Lay the chicken on a sheet pan and sprinkle both sides with salt and pepper.

2. Heat the olive oil in a large skillet over medium-high heat. Add the chicken . . .

3. And cook until the surface is golden and crisp, 2 to 3 minutes per side. (The chicken won't quite be cooked through.)

4. Remove it to a plate . . .

5. Then add the onion and garlic to the skillet . . .

6. And cook, stirring, until the onion is softened, about 3 minutes.

The color is as fab
as the flavor!

7. Add the turmeric and stir it in. (Be aware: A little goes a long way!)

8. Then add the rice . . .

9. 1½ cups water . . .

10. And the jar of mango salsa! Stir it in . . .

11. Then add the chili powder and stir it in. Lookin' good!

12. Return the chicken to the pan, along with the juices on the plate.

13. Put the lid on the pan, reduce the heat to low, and simmer until the rice is tender and the chicken is cooked through, 18 to 20 minutes.

14. Use a large serving spoon to grab a piece of chicken with lots of saucy rice . . .

15. And serve it with cilantro leaves and lime wedges.

~~~~~~~~~~~~~~~~~~

VARIATIONS

- *Use regular jarred salsa instead of mango salsa.*
- *Serve with guacamole and sour cream.*
- *Use peach salsa for another sweet option!*

Ladd and his BFFs!

CHICKEN WITH ROASTED RED PEPPER SAUCE

 35 MINUTES **MAKES 6 SERVINGS**

I have used, loved, cooked with, and eaten jarred roasted red peppers for years, and next to canned tomatoes, I'd consider them one of the most versatile pantry items in the universe. You can eat them whole as a snack, you can layer them in a sandwich or panini, and you can chop them and put them on cream cheese for a yummy appetizer. But this simple sauce, which I originally made for pasta years ago, is positively spectacular, and it celebrates all that is wonderful about the flavor of RRPs! (I use them so much that I have to abbreviate sometimes!!) Once you try this, you'll make it time and time and time again.

6 chicken breast cutlets

Kosher salt and ground black pepper

1 tablespoon Italian seasoning

4 tablespoons olive oil

2 tablespoons butter

½ large yellow onion, finely diced

4 garlic cloves, minced

One 15.5-ounce jar roasted red peppers, drained and roughly chopped

1½ cups low-sodium vegetable or chicken broth

½ cup heavy cream

Shaved Parmesan cheese, for serving

Chopped fresh basil, for serving

1. Put the chicken in a plastic storage bag or bowl. Add a generous pinch of salt and pepper, the Italian seasoning, and 3 tablespoons of the olive oil.

2. Seal the bag and smush it all around to mix, then set it aside while you start on the sauce.

3. Heat the butter and remaining 1 tablespoon olive oil in a large skillet over medium heat, then add the onion and garlic . . .

4. And cook, stirring, until they start to soften, about 3 minutes.

5. Add the roasted red peppers . . .

6. And cook until the peppers are piping hot, about 3 minutes.

7. Add the broth . . .

8. And a pinch of salt and pepper . . .

9. And cook for 2 to 3 minutes, until heated through.

10. Add the cream . . .

11. And bring it to a gentle boil. Reduce the heat to low and let it simmer for 5 minutes, until the flavors have developed well. Turn off the heat and let the sauce cool a bit while you work on the chicken.

12. Heat a large skillet over medium-high heat and add the chicken. Let it cook for 3 to 4 minutes on one side.

13. Meanwhile, transfer the sauce to a blender or food processor . . .

14. And very carefully pulse to puree. *Important*: Blending hot food can be dangerous, so do not blend when the sauce is piping hot, and do not turn on the blender full speed. Blend in short pulses to make sure the sauce doesn't expand and splash.

15. Pour the sauce back into the skillet and let it simmer over low heat while you finish cooking the chicken. Taste and adjust the seasonings, making sure to salt it adequately!

16. Turn the chicken over and cook it on the other side until it's cooked through, about 3 minutes.

17. Serve pieces of chicken with a good amount of sauce over the top! Shave on Parmesan cheese and sprinkle on a little basil.

VARIATIONS

- *Serve over pasta.*
- *Stir 2 tablespoons of pesto into the sauce as it simmers.*
- *Serve the sauce with a medium-rare steak! OMG.*
- *Add 2 teaspoons red pepper flakes for a nice, hot version.*

Page 298!

The easiest, tastiest sauce!

Steak Suppers

To begin this chapter, I'd like to state the obvious: *Steaks are just too freaking good.* And I'm not just saying that because I'm married to a cattle rancher! (Do you believe me? Ha ha.) But seriously, friends. When seasoned, cooked, and served right, a simple steak really doesn't require much adornment, accompaniment, or fuss. Unlike chicken or pork, which (it can be argued) need a lot going on to make it exciting, a medium-rare steak stands proudly on its inherent flavor and beautiful, juicy texture. On a practical level, steak is versatile! It can be the basis of a casual supper around the grill outside or an elegant candlelit dinner! The following is a collection of some of my go-to steak suppers of late, and I think you'll love how each one celebrates the concept of "steak" in a different way. I'll end by repeating the obvious: *Steaks are just too freaking good!*

FAMILY-STYLE RIB-EYE SANDWICHES

🕐 25 MINUTES **MAKES 4 TO 6 SERVINGS**

Family-style sandwiches seem like an obvious concept, but I'm a relatively late adopter. However, I'm more than making up for it in recent months, as I have 100 percent hopped on board the family-style sandwich train! Now, just to be clear: I'm not talking about foot-long or even twelve-foot-long regular submarine sandwiches or hoagies. What I'm talking about is building an oversize sandwich using oversize bread (and oversize flavors!), then slicing it into more reasonable (and socially acceptable) sizes.

Still unsure? Check out this big, bodacious rib-eye version. I promise you'll wanna hop on the train with me! I'll scooch over. There's plenty of room!

⅓ cup mayonnaise

¼ cup sour cream

⅓ cup pickled jalapeño slices

Several dashes jalapeño hot sauce

2 tablespoons prepared pesto

Kosher salt and ground black pepper

2 large rib-eye steaks, about 1½ inches thick

3 tablespoons Montreal steak seasoning

4 tablespoons olive oil

1 large ciabatta loaf

2 cups baby arugula

¼ cup Pickled Red Onions (page 14)

1. First, make the spread so the flavors can start to marry: Combine the mayonnaise, sour cream, half the jalapeños, the hot sauce, pesto, and a pinch of salt and pepper in a food processor or blender.

2. Process or blend until everything is green and wonderful, then set it aside.

4. Then drizzle the steaks with 2 tablespoons of the olive oil.

3. Preheat a grill pan or cast-iron skillet over medium-high heat. Season the steaks on both sides with the steak seasoning . . .

5. Add the steaks to the grill pan and cook until medium-rare, about 4 minutes per side.

Slice it thick or thin to suit your needs!

Pickled Red Onions
(page 14)

6. Remove them to a tray or plate, cover them lightly with foil, and set them aside to rest.

7. Split the ciabatta loaf in half . . .

8. And drizzle the cut sides with the remaining 2 tablespoons olive oil. Lay the pieces on the grill pan cut side down, pressing firmly so they absorb the juices from the pan.

9. Grill the bread for about 5 minutes, pressing occasionally, until the surface is crisp and the edges are starting to char.

10. Slice the steaks into thin strips.

11. Divide the herby spread between the 2 halves of the bread (it will feel like a lot, but the sandwich will thank you for it!) and spread it all over.

12. Pile on the steak. (Ditto my thoughts above! It's a lot, but this is for a whole family, man!)

13. Pile on the arugula (I am sensing a theme here) . . .

14. Then top with the red onions and the rest of the jalapeños!

15. Slice the sandwich in half using a serrated knife, then keep slicing the halves in half according to how many bodies you need to feed!

VARIATIONS

- *If you like a cold sandwich, wrap the whole sandwich tightly in plastic wrap after assembling and refrigerate it for a couple of hours or up to 12 hours. Then just slice to serve. Perfect for a picnic!*
- *Replace the herby spread with Honey Chipotle Crema (page 24).*
- *Add a layer of pepper Jack cheese slices on top of the sliced steak.*
- *Substitute chicken breasts for the steak!*

HERBY SKIRT STEAK WITH SWEET POTATO FRIES

🕐 30 MINUTES **MAKES 4 SERVINGS**

In my cooking life these days, I've settled into a blissfully sustainable groove where I'll combine an easy shortcut ingredient with a nice from-scratch element or two. Nothing more perfectly illustrates this best-of-both-worlds spot I've carved out for myself than this steak dinner, which combines frozen fries with a homemade herb sauce in what is a truly gorgeous plate of food! Skirt steak is perfect for this meal, because the flavor is through the roof and it takes just a few minutes to cook up perfectly. Oh me oh my, I am lovin' this recipe!

Kosher salt and ground black pepper

1 teaspoon ground cumin

½ teaspoon ground coriander

½ teaspoon dried oregano

¼ teaspoon cayenne pepper

Pinch of sugar

1 skirt steak (about 2 pounds), cut into 4 smaller steaks

One 20-ounce bag frozen sweet potato fries

¾ cup olive oil

¼ cup chopped fresh cilantro

¼ cup chopped fresh parsley

2 tablespoons chopped fresh oregano

1 garlic clove, grated

½ teaspoon red pepper flakes

3 tablespoons red wine vinegar

1. Preheat the oven to 425°F.

2. In a small bowl, stir together 2 teaspoons kosher salt, 1 teaspoon pepper, the cumin, coriander, oregano, cayenne, and sugar.

3. Sprinkle both sides of the steaks with half of the seasoning mix and set them aside while you preheat a grill pan or cast-iron skillet over medium-high heat.

4. Spread the sweet potato fries on a sheet pan and sprinkle on the rest of the seasoning mix. Toss to coat. Bake the fries until golden, 25 to 30 minutes, tossing them halfway through.

An herby and scrumptiously
simple steak supper!

5. Drizzle ¼ cup of the olive oil on the steaks and grill them on one side for about 3 minutes, or until good grill marks form.

6. Flip them over and cook for another 2 to 3 minutes for medium-rare. Remove the steaks to a plate to rest.

7. Sprinkle the herbs into a medium bowl . . .

8. And add the garlic, pepper flakes, and a pinch of salt and pepper.

9. Splash in the vinegar . . .

10. And stir as you drizzle in the remaining ½ cup olive oil.

11. Clear out four spaces among the fries and place the steaks on the pan.

12. Drizzle the pan juices over the steaks—you don't want to waste that flavor!

13. Spoon on the herb sauce and serve!

TIP

- If there's extra herb drizzle, stir it into a little sour cream and buttermilk to make a salad dressing (or dipping sauce for the fries!).

Yes, this passes as a salad in my world!

STEAK FRITES SALAD

Here's how my twisted mind works: One day I decided to make a salad. Then I decided to make a steak to serve on the salad. Then I thought the steak needed a sauce, so I made a batch of hollandaise. Then I looked at the steak and it made me think of steak frites, so I decided to bring fries into the whole thing. And when it was all said and done, I decided not to budge from the whole "salad" designation. I love my twisted mind!

This looks like a mighty elaborate undertaking, but if you get all your ducks in a row before you start, you can have it on the table in thirty-ish minutes! Not bad for a darn delectable, showstopping *salad*! (I told you I wasn't budging.)

One 28-ounce bag frozen fries

1¼ cups (2½ sticks) butter, melted

2 tablespoons chopped fresh rosemary

Kosher salt

2 tablespoons coarsely ground black pepper, plus more as needed

2 New York strip steaks

⅓ cup olive oil, plus more for the steaks

3 egg yolks

Juice of 2 lemons, plus more to taste

Dash of hot sauce

4 cups packed salad greens (I used a spring mix)

⅓ cup Pickled Red Onions (page 14) or sliced raw red onion

½ cup halved grape tomatoes

1. Preheat the oven according to the frozen fries package.

2. Spread the fries on a sheet pan and drizzle ¼ cup of the melted butter on top.

4. Toss to coat all the fries, then bake them according to the package directions (usually 20 to 25 minutes).

6. And press the steaks into the black pepper to coat the surface on both sides.

3. Sprinkle on the rosemary and a pinch of salt and pepper.

5. Meanwhile, sprinkle 2 tablespoons of coarse black pepper on a sheet pan or plate. Season the steaks on both sides with a generous pinch of salt . . .

7. Preheat a grill pan or cast-iron skillet over medium-high heat. Drizzle both sides of the steaks with olive oil.

8. Place the steaks on the grill or in the pan . . .

9. And cook, flipping them halfway through, until medium-rare, 4 to 5 minutes per side. Remove them to a board and lightly cover them with foil to rest.

10. Add the egg yolks to a blender . . .

11. And add the juice of 1 lemon. Meanwhile, heat the rest of the melted butter so that it's sizzling hot.

12. Blend the egg yolks and lemon juice for a few seconds, then turn the blender on low speed and very slowly drizzle in the hot melted butter. You will hear it start to thicken!

13. Add a few dashes of hot sauce and blend for a few more seconds.

14. Check out the hollandaise! Give it a little taste and add salt if it needs it. If it's overly thick, squeeze in a little more lemon juice and blend, or blend in a tablespoon or two of hot water.

15. Make the dressing: In a small pitcher, mix the remaining juice of 1 lemon, the olive oil, and a pinch of salt and pepper.

16. Arrange the greens on a platter or in a large wide bowl and drizzle on some of the dressing.

17. Sprinkle on half the fries. (You'll serve the rest on the side!)

18. Then slice the steaks . . .

19. And arrange the pieces over the top of the salad.

20. You know what's next! Drizzle half of the hollandaise all over the steaks. (You'll serve the rest on the side with the fries.)

21. Top with pickled red onions and tomatoes. Serve with the rest of the fries and hollandaise and be transported to paradise.

Fred and his person!

A sensational spin on a steakhouse classic!

T-BONE STEAK WITH CREAMED GREENS

⏱ 30 MINUTES **MAKES 2 TO 4 SERVINGS**

Do you have a list of "Last Supper" dishes—the foods you'd choose to eat if you knew it was your last meal in this earthly realm? Well, I do. And rather than cycle my preferences in and out through the years I have simply added items to the point that my final meal will take about nine days to finish. What can I say, I love life and I want to stretch it out as long as possible!

Anyway, one component of my last supper wish list has always been a medium-rare steak with creamed spinach. It's a steakhouse staple of mine, and in recent years I've been spiking the spinach with different greens to really drive home the vitamin A (and C and K and so on) goodness. Because, of course, the only reason I make this dinner is for the greens . . . ahem.

---

2 tablespoons salted butter

2 tablespoons olive oil

2 T-bone steaks

Kosher salt and ground black pepper

1 large yellow onion, thinly sliced

3 garlic cloves, sliced

½ teaspoon red pepper flakes

⅓ cup white wine

⅓ cup heavy cream

2 cups thinly sliced collard greens, stems removed

2 cups thinly sliced kale, stems removed

2 cups spinach, stems removed

1½ cups grated fontina cheese

Fresh (old school–style!) curly parsley, for garnish

Lemon wedges, for serving

---

1. Preheat the broiler.

2. Heat the butter and olive oil in a large cast-iron skillet over medium-high heat. Season the steaks on both sides with salt and pepper and add them to the pan.

3. Cook the steaks, moving them around the pan frequently, until medium-rare, 3 to 4 minutes per side.

4. Remove the steaks to a tray or plate to rest, lightly covering them with foil to keep them warm.

5. Add the onion, garlic, and pepper flakes to the pan . . .

6. And cook, stirring frequently, until the onion is softened, about 3 minutes.

7. Pour in the wine, then stir and let it reduce for about 1 minute. (The pan will still be nice and hot!)

8. Pour in the cream and stir . . .

9. Then add the mountain of greens! You can add them in handfuls, stirring them in as you go, or just do what I do and go for it all at once!

10. Reduce the heat to low and use tongs to fold in the greens.

11. They'll start to wilt quickly!

12. When the greens are mostly wilted, turn off the heat and arrange them in an even layer. Sprinkle on the fontina . . .

13. Then place the pan under the broiler until the cheese is melted and creamy. Should take less than 2 minutes!

14. Serve up each steak with a generous portion of greens . . .

15. And garnish with parsley and lemon!

~~~~~~~~~~~~~~~~~~~~

VARIATIONS

- *Skip the grated cheese and serve the greens in the cream sauce. Still very yummy!*
- *Use any cut of steak you like: sirloin, rib eye, strip, even filet if you're feeling fancy!*

Steak Diane

⏱ 20 MINUTES MAKES 4 SERVINGS

I included this extravagant, indulgent dish in this cookbook because, well, it's extravagant and indulgent. It's most certainly a dinner you'll want to make for your sweetie and kids on graduation night, or for friends celebrating an anniversary, or for the president of the United States, or . . . okay. It's really not that extravagant! (By the way, here's a dinnertime question for you to pose to the table: If you could have anyone in the history of the world drop by your place for a surprise dinner, who would you choose?)

Steak Diane is a classic! Its brandy cream sauce is outta sight, and it really comes together quickly! And I wish I had a plate of it in front of me right now. Because after all, "now" is always a special occasion.

(My drop-in dinner guest would be Jimmy Stewart, by the way. I'd marry him today if I could. Ladd would understand!)

Four 6-ounce filet mignon steaks

Kosher salt and ground black pepper

1 tablespoon olive oil

1 tablespoon salted butter

1 shallot, finely chopped (or sub ½ cup finely chopped yellow onion)

2 garlic cloves, minced

¼ cup brandy

¼ cup low-sodium beef broth

¼ cup heavy cream

1 tablespoon Dijon mustard

1 teaspoon Worcestershire sauce

Chopped fresh parsley, for garnish

Chopped fresh chives, for garnish

1. Flatten the steaks with a mallet until they're ¾ to 1 inch thick.

2. Sprinkle both sides with a generous pinch of salt and pepper.

3. Heat the olive oil and butter in a large cast-iron skillet over medium-high heat. Add the steaks and cook for 2½ minutes on one side . . .

4. Then flip them over and cook for about 2 minutes on the other side for medium-rare. Cook them a little longer if you like more doneness.

5. Remove the steaks to a platter and lightly cover them with foil to rest.

6. Add the shallot and garlic to the skillet and stir them around for 1 minute, scraping the pan as you go.

Page 298!

Serve this to your VIPs!

7. Turn off the heat, then pour in the brandy. Let it simmer, stirring often, for 1 minute . . .

8. Then carefully turn the heat to medium.

9. Add the broth . . .

10. The cream . . .

11. And the mustard.

12. Stir and add the Worcestershire . . .

13. Then let the sauce cook for a couple of minutes, until slightly thickened.

14. Pour the sauce all over the steaks . . .

15. Then sprinkle on the parsley and chives. Serve immediately to special people in your life!

~~~~~~~~~~

VARIATION

• *Use any steak, from sirloin to rib eye! The sauce is delicious on any beef.*

"Steak WHO?!?"

RETRO SALISBURY STEAKS

🕐 25 MINUTES **MAKES 4 SERVINGS**

Oh, do I ever love Salisbury steak. It takes me back to so many places: Watching *The Brady Bunch*. Eating it while watching *The Brady Bunch*. Eating it while dreaming of Peter Brady while watching *The Brady Bunch*. Did I just say that out loud? Oops! (But Peter was definitely the best brother. Who's with me on this??)

I've made many variations of this beloved old-fashioned favorite of the '60s and '70s, and I'd say this one's my current favorite because of the naughty tastiness (and naughty convenience) of French onion soup mix. Such a simple thing to pull together—artificial grill marks and all! (Read the recipe and you'll see what I mean.)

1½ pounds lean ground beef

½ cup seasoned breadcrumbs

One 1-ounce packet French onion soup mix

4 dashes of Worcestershire sauce

4 tablespoons barbecue sauce

Kosher salt and ground black pepper

1 tablespoon olive oil

1 tablespoon salted butter

1 generous tablespoon all-purpose flour

¼ cup sherry or white wine

1½ cups low-sodium beef broth

Fresh parsley leaves, for garnish

1. In a large bowl, combine the ground beef, breadcrumbs, half of the French onion soup mix . . .

3. Use your hands to smush all the ingredients together.

5. And use the back of a dinner knife to form 4 or 5 "grill" marks on one side of each steak.

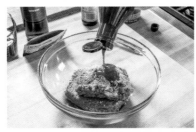

2. The Worcestershire, 2 tablespoons of the barbecue sauce, and a pinch of salt and pepper.

4. Form 8 small oval patties . . .

6. Heat the olive oil and butter in a large skillet over medium heat and add the steaks, "grill" marks side down. Cook for 5 minutes on one side.

1971 called; they
want their recipe back!

7. Flip them to the other side and cook them until no longer pink in the middle, another 3 to 4 minutes. You want the surface to be really deep in color to resemble a grilled steak.

8. Remove the steaks to a tray and pour off all but 3 tablespoons of the grease from the skillet (if there is more than that). Reduce the heat to medium-low and sprinkle in the flour.

9. Whisk the flour into the fat to form a paste, scraping as much off the bottom of the pan as you can. Let it cook for about 2 minutes until the roux gets deep golden . . .

10. Then pour in the sherry . . .

11. The broth . . .

12. And the rest of the French onion soup mix.

13. Add the remaining 2 tablespoons barbecue sauce and whisk to combine, then raise the heat to medium and bring to a gentle boil. Cook until thickened, 4 to 5 minutes.

14. Turn the heat to low and return the steaks to the sauce. Spoon the sauce over the steaks and let the steaks simmer for a couple of minutes as you keep basting them. Serve one to two steaks per person with a sprinkle of parsley.

VARIATIONS

- *After you remove the steaks, add 8 ounces sliced mushrooms to the skillet and cook them for 5 minutes before moving forward with the sauce.*
- *Serve the steaks and sauce over mashed potatoes or egg noodles!*

STEAK MEDALLIONS WITH BABY POTATOES

🕐 30 MINUTES   **MAKES 4 TO 6 SERVINGS**

Question—and I want you to dig deep in your soul for the answer. To keep things fair, I'm going to try to ask the question in the most impartial language I can muster. Would you rather have a boring, run-of-the-mill, dreadfully pitiful and ordinary steak and baked potato for dinner . . . or delightful little medallions of beef, seasoned perfectly and served over a bountiful bed of smashed baby potatoes and an herby sautéed onion topping? Go ahead and think about it. I'll wait!

(By the way, lest you think my fancy words mean anything at all, Ladd's answer would definitely be "Steak and baked potato, please." He is immune to my flowery descriptions!)

1½ pounds bite-size potatoes
(Baby Golds or similar)

Kosher salt

2 rib-eye steaks, about 1 inch thick

2 tablespoons Montreal steak seasoning

2 tablespoons butter

2 tablespoons olive oil

1 large yellow onion, thinly sliced

2 tablespoons minced garlic

1 tablespoon fresh oregano leaves

1 teaspoon fresh thyme leaves

⅓ cup white wine

2 teaspoons flaky sea salt

Chopped fresh parsley, for garnish

Bottled horseradish sauce, for serving (optional)

1. Get the potatoes going by putting them in a sauté pan of water over medium-high heat. Add a generous pinch of salt and cook until the potatoes are fork-tender, 12 to 14 minutes.

2. Trim the excess fat from the outside of each steak, then cut each one into 4 smaller "medallions."

3. Sprinkle the steak seasoning on both sides of the medallions.

4. Heat the butter and oil in a heavy skillet over medium-high heat, then add the steaks to the pan. Cook them for about 3 minutes on one side . . .

For the meat-and-potato
people in your life!

5. Then turn them over, cooking them for another 3 minutes for medium-rare. Remove the steaks to a tray or plate. (Psst. Lightly cover the steaks to keep them warm!)

6. Add the onion, garlic, oregano, and thyme to the skillet.

7. Stir and cook until the onion is soft and deep golden, 6 to 7 minutes.

8. Add the wine, then stir and let it reduce for about 1 minute. Reduce the heat to low.

9. Put the potatoes on a large platter and use the bottom of a sturdy glass (or a metal measuring cup) to smash the potatoes into flattened discs.

10. Sprinkle the potatoes with the flaky sea salt . . .

11. Then pour the onion mixture all over the potatoes, trying to cover most of them in the process.

12. Arrange the steaks all over the top . . .

13. And sprinkle with the minced parsley. If you'd like, serve with horseradish sauce on the side.

~~~~~~

VARIATIONS

- *Skip the baby potatoes and put the onions and steaks over Instant Cheesy Mash (page 311) or your favorite baked potatoes.*
- *Use red wine instead of white for a richer onion mixture.*

Pizza Party

Pizza has officially taken over the universe. It's pretty much like air at this point, as it is absolutely everywhere. You can make it for dinner. You can eat it for lunch. You can whip up a breakfast pizza. Or you can eat last night's leftover pizza for breakfast! You can eat pizza as an appetizer or a midnight snack. And here's the thing about pizza: It's simply a matter of "what kind," never about "whether." After all, everyone loves pizza, including Ladd, Alex, Mauricio, Paige, Bryce, Jamar, Todd, me, and every person I know and don't know. So here is a new batch of splendiferous pizza recipes you will absolutely fall in love with, as well as a revisiting of my favorite-of-all-time pizza crust, which makes any topping sing opera! If you've found yourself relying on take-out pizza lately, friends, lean back into making pizza yourself. You'll fall in love again!

READY-TO-GO PIZZA DOUGH

⏱ 10 MINUTES (PLUS 2 HOURS TO RISE)

MAKES ABOUT 2 POUNDS (ENOUGH FOR 2 PIZZAS)

As someone who's passionate about simple, easy (and yes, fast!) cooking, I'll admit that I sometimes settle into grooves of store-bought or ready-made ingredients and forget to go back to the originals here and there. Pizza dough is the perfect example: While I love using store-bought pizza dough, frozen bread dough, even canned biscuit dough for pizza, anytime I take the extra time to use my original from-scratch pizza dough, I always scold myself for staying away so long. You can't beat the flavor, the chew, and the texture of homemade dough, and this one's foolproof! It takes a little time, but if you make one at the beginning of the week, you can keep it in the fridge and have it at the ready whenever the pizza mood strikes! (And trust me, it will strike.)

1 teaspoon instant or active dry yeast

1½ cups warm water

4 cups all-purpose flour

1 teaspoon kosher salt

⅓ cup olive oil, plus more for coating the bowl

1. Sprinkle the yeast over the warm water in a small pitcher. The water should be quite a bit warmer than lukewarm but not hot to the touch. Let it stand for 5 minutes without stirring.

2. Add the flour and salt to the bowl of a stand mixer . . .

3. Then turn the mixer on low and slowly drizzle in the olive oil.

4. Give the yeast mixture a stir, then slowly add it while the mixer is running.

5. Let the dough mix for 2 minutes, until smooth.

6. Drizzle some olive oil in a large bowl and add the dough, turning it to coat it in the oil.

7. Cover the bowl with plastic wrap and set it aside in a warm, draft-free spot for 2 hours to rise. It should double in size!

8. Divide the dough in half and use it right away (this recipe makes 2 standard pizza crusts!) or pop the bowl in the fridge for up to 4 days. If it rises too much, just punch it down from time to time. The flavor develops over the 4 days, so experiment with when you like it best! (It's delicious anytime.)

SHORTCUT CRUSTS!

No time to make dough? Use English muffins, flour tortillas, canned biscuits, halved deli rolls, halved croissants (press them flat!), crescent roll dough, focaccia, or halved ciabatta loaves! Viva la pizza!

The only pizza dough you'll ever need!

You can't beat
this classic!

CAST-IRON HAMBURGER PIZZA

🕐 30 MINUTES **MAKES 1 PIZZA, TO SERVE 4 TO 6**

I'm guilty of this, too, but there are so many fancy schmancy, nouvelle cuisine, frilly gourmet pizzas out there that sometimes we forget where we came from. This hamburger pizza is where I came from, and no amount of fig and prosciutto can erase how positively splendid it is when all you're looking for is some dang bread, meat, and cheese in pizza form. I make it in a cast-iron skillet to really crisp up the edges, and don't worry: For this pizza there'll be no sprinkling of hamburger fixins like shredded lettuce and tomato on top. This one sings simplicity, and it's one of my favorite tunes ever.

½ **pound ground beef**

Kosher salt and ground black pepper

4 **tablespoons olive oil**

1 **pound (½ batch) Ready-to-Go Pizza Dough (page 208)**

½ **cup marinara sauce**

1 **generous cup grated mozzarella cheese**

1. Preheat the oven to 500°F. (Try the convection setting if you have it!)

2. Heat a 12-inch cast-iron skillet over medium-high heat and add the ground beef. Add a pinch of salt and pepper . . .

3. And cook the meat, crumbling it as fine as you can, until it's fully cooked, 4 to 5 minutes.

4. Pour the meat into a bowl and wipe out the pan with a paper towel.

5. Return the skillet to the stovetop over medium heat. Drizzle in 2 tablespoons of the olive oil . . .

6. And lay the pizza dough in the skillet, stretching it out to the edges. If it's too springy, let it sit for 15 minutes and try again.

7. Spread the marinara sauce over the dough, leaving a ½-inch border. Sprinkle half the mozzarella over the sauce . . .

Fred and Rusty make our empty nest less boring!

8. Then sprinkle the beef over the cheese.

9. Add the rest of the cheese (this will sort of "protect" the beef and keep it from getting too crisp) and sprinkle on a pinch of salt and pepper.

10. Drizzle the remaining 2 tablespoons olive oil all around the edge of the crust, letting it coat the crust and drip over the outer edge of the crust.

11. Bake until the cheese is bubbly and the crust is deep golden, 12 to 14 minutes. Cut into wedges and serve immediately.

RAINBOW PIZZA

⏱ 30 MINUTES **MAKES 1 PIZZA, TO SERVE 6 TO 8**

A veggie pizza is always a treat, especially when the veggies form a beautiful, edible rainbow! This pretty pizza is a double whammy of wonderfulness: The presentation is stunning, and the piles of roasted veggies are delicious beyond description. Cut it into very small squares so everyone can get a taste of this or that, or split the sections according to vegetable. So fun!

1 pound (½ batch) Ready-to-Go Pizza Dough (page 208)

½ cup marinara sauce

1½ cups grated mozzarella cheese

1 small red onion, finely diced

6 spears asparagus, ends trimmed, cut into ½-inch pieces

Kernels from 1 ear corn (or ½ cup frozen corn)

1 orange bell pepper, thinly sliced

⅓ cup halved red cherry tomatoes

1 teaspoon Italian seasoning

Kosher salt and ground black pepper

Olive oil, for brushing

Basil leaves, for garnish

1. Preheat the oven to 500°F. (Try the convection setting if you have it!)

2. Stretch out the dough on a sheet pan to form a large oval. If it's too springy, let it sit for 15 minutes and try again.

3. Spread on the sauce, leaving a ½-inch border.

4. Sprinkle on the mozzarella . . .

5. Then arrange all the veggies in sections . . .

6. Until you've created a rainbow!

7. Sprinkle on the Italian seasoning, along with a pinch of salt and pepper . . .

We go on a date every four years or so!

8. Then brush the crust with olive oil.

9. Bake until the vegetables are nice and roasted and the crust is golden, 13 to 15 minutes. Top with torn basil leaves, then cut into squares to serve.

DATE NIGHTS ARE EASIER

After raising kids for over two decades, Ladd and I have discovered a whole new benefit now that the nest is empty. Without teenagers to manage (and monitor), we can hop in the truck at a moment's notice and go paint the town red anytime we want! (Okay, we've done it once in the ten months Todd's been gone. But give us time!!)

Every slice is different!

SPINACH ARTICHOKE PIZZA

30 MINUTES **MAKES 1 THICK-CRUST PIZZA, TO SERVE 8 TO 12**

In my years of cooking and eating (and what a bunch of years it's been), I've determined that the whole spinach-artichoke theme works with pretty much everything under the sun. Dip, naturally. Pasta, you bet. Grilled cheese, oh yes! And pizza? Well, it's an absolute no-brainer. This celebrates the creamy wonderfulness of spinach-artichoke everything, with big garlic flavor to boot. Make this part of your pizza rotation . . . pronto. You won't be sorry!

¼ cup prepared pesto

6 or 7 cloves Garlic Confit (page 3), or 3 raw cloves pressed in a garlic press

1 tablespoon olive oil

5 cups packed baby spinach

Kosher salt and ground black pepper

2 pounds Ready-to-Go Pizza Dough (page 208)

1 cup grated mozzarella cheese

1 cup grated fontina cheese

1 cup canned artichokes, drained and partly chopped (leave some artichoke "rosettes" intact)

Pinch of red pepper flakes

Grated Parmesan cheese, for serving

Fresh basil leaves, for garnish

1. Preheat the oven to 500°F. (Try the convection setting if you have it!)

2. In a small bowl, combine the pesto and garlic . . .

3. And stir, mashing the garlic as you go.

4. Heat the olive oil in a large skillet over medium heat and add the spinach along with a pinch of salt and pepper.

5. Cook and wilt the spinach for about 2 minutes. If the spinach is very wet, drain it on paper towels.

6. Stretch the dough onto a sheet pan. If it's too springy, let it sit for 15 minutes and try again. Spread the pesto mix all over, leaving a ½-inch border and a small amount of the pesto mix in the bowl.

7. Arrange the spinach all over the pesto . . .

Garlic Confit
(page 3)

The crust itself is a total treat!

8. Then sprinkle on the mozzarella and fontina and arrange the artichokes all over the top.

9. Sprinkle on a pinch of red pepper flakes, then brush the remaining pesto mix all around the outer crust. Power move here! That crust will have amazing flavor.

10. Bake the pizza until the cheese is bubbly and the crust is golden, 16 to 18 minutes. Sprinkle on Parmesan and add torn basil leaves. Cut into squares and serve.

VARIATIONS

- Add a thin layer of marinara or pizza sauce after spreading on the pesto mixture.
- Add thin slices of prosciutto to the pizza before sprinkling on the cheese.
- Dot the top of the pizza with crumbled goat cheese as soon as it comes out of the oven.

"Wanna go for a *ride*?!?"

My MOM'S FRIEND'S HUSBAND'S WHITE CLAM PIZZA

⏱ 30 MINUTES **MAKES 1 PIZZA, TO SERVE 6 TO 8**

I love being surprised by food! My mom, who is a prolific home cook, raved and raved to me for the longest time about this pizza, which was first made for her by the husband of a buddy of hers in Connecticut. As daughters sometimes do with their mothers, I shrugged it off and ignored it anytime she'd bring it up, until the day she asserted herself and finally foisted her friend's husband's recipe upon me. The result was positively out of this world, through the roof, and beyond comprehension. I was (and continue to be) positively bowled over by how magnificent this is! Don't be like me and wait forever. This is a pizza you need in your life!

One 6.5-ounce can good-quality chopped clams

3 garlic cloves, pressed in a garlic press

1 teaspoon red pepper flakes, plus more for garnish

Kosher salt and ground black pepper

1 teaspoon chopped fresh oregano, plus more for garnish

2 tablespoons olive oil, plus more for brushing and the pan

1 pound (½ batch) Ready-to-Go Pizza Dough (page 208)

¾ cup grated low-moisture mozzarella cheese

¼ cup grated Pecorino Romano cheese

1. Preheat the oven to 475°F. (Try the convection setting if you have it!)

2. Drain the clams over a bowl.

3. Put the clams in a separate bowl and add 3 tablespoons of the clam juice, discarding the rest.

4. Add the garlic . . .

5. The pepper flakes, and a pinch of salt and black pepper.

6. Add the oregano and olive oil . . .

7. And stir to mix.

8. Stretch the pizza dough into a large oval on a well-oiled sheet pan. If it's too springy, let it sit for 15 minutes and try again.

9. Brush olive oil all over the top of the dough . . .

10. Sprinkle with salt and pepper . . .

11. And sprinkle on the mozzarella and half of the Romano cheese, leaving about a 1-inch border.

12. Sprinkle the clam mixture on top . . .

13. Then bake the pizza until the crust is golden and crisp around the edges and the cheese is starting to turn golden, 15 to 18 minutes. Garnish with chopped oregano, pepper flakes, and the remaining Romano. Cut it into squares and serve immediately.

VARIATION

• *Add a few garlic confit cloves (page 3) to the top of the pizza before baking.*

Brothers, coworkers, friends!

Best pizza I've had in
the past five years.
No joke!

If my heart and soul are feeling out of whack,
this is what puts them back on track.

GRILLED VEGGIE AND PROSCIUTTO PITA PIZZA

⏱ 30 MINUTES **MAKES 2 PERSONAL PIZZAS**

There are no lengths I won't go to in order to eat pizza, and I've been known to turn anything remotely resembling bread into a pizza crust. From English muffins to tortillas, no bread is safe from my shenanigans, and that's part of what makes the whole world of pizza so fun. In all my experimentation (born of desperation?), there's one easy-to-grab supermarket staple that especially stands out . . . and that's pita bread! I was skeptical when I first gave it a try, but I loved it immediately and I've been giving it a try regularly ever since. This veggie-and-prosciutto version is positively to die for, with big pesto flavor and grilled veggies everywhere you turn!

2 tablespoons olive oil

2 garlic cloves, grated

4 tablespoons prepared pesto

1 teaspoon minced fresh oregano

Kosher salt and ground black pepper

2 whole-wheat pita breads

6 asparagus spears, ends trimmed

1 small yellow squash, trimmed and halved lengthwise

2 mini sweet peppers

1 shallot, peeled and halved lengthwise

4 prosciutto slices

2 ounces goat cheese

Fresh basil leaves, for serving

Balsamic glaze, for serving

1. In a bowl, stir together the olive oil, garlic, 2 tablespoons of the pesto, oregano, and a pinch of salt and pepper.

4. To the pesto mixture remaining in the bowl, add the asparagus, squash, peppers, and shallots . . .

2. Brush one-quarter of the pesto mixture on both sides of the pita breads.

3. And toss to coat the veggies in the mixture.

Pita makes a perfect pizza crust!

5. Heat a grill pan over medium heat and add the veggies. Grill them for 5 minutes or so . . .

6. Then turn them over and grill the other side for 4 minutes or so, until good grill marks form. Remove them to a board and let them cool for a few minutes.

7. Put the pitas on the grill pan and grill them until you get nice grill marks on both sides, 3 to 4 minutes per side.

8. Chop the veggies into bite-size pieces.

9. Spread the remaining 2 tablespoons pesto over both pieces of pita . . .

10. Then arrange 1 slice of prosciutto on each half of both pitas . . .

11. And pile on the vegetables!

12. Add some crumbles of goat cheese . . .

13. Then add basil leaves and drizzle with balsamic glaze. Cut it into wedges!

MEATY PITA PIZZA

🕐 15 MINUTES **MAKES 2 PERSONAL PIZZAS**

This pita pizza uses both the grill pan and the broiler for a best-of-both worlds pizza scenario! This meaty, cheesy version is perfect for teenagers, cowboys, college football players . . . and basically everyone.

2 pita breads

2 tablespoons olive oil, plus more for brushing the pitas

1 mounded tablespoon prepared pesto

¼ cup marinara sauce

2 garlic cloves, grated

Kosher salt and ground black pepper

1 cup grated mozzarella cheese

4 extra-large pepperoni slices

½ orange bell pepper, cut into thin strips

¼ cup mini pepperoni

2 tablespoons sliced black olives

1 green onion, sliced, for serving

Red pepper flakes, for serving

Grated Parmesan, for serving

1. Preheat the broiler.

2. Preheat a grill pan over medium heat and generously brush both sides of the pitas with olive oil.

3. Start grilling the pitas, pressing them into the grates on the grill.

4. While the first side is grilling, make a sauce by combining 1 tablespoon of the olive oil, the pesto, marinara sauce, garlic, and a pinch of salt and pepper in a medium bowl.

5. Stir to mix it all together.

6. When the first side has gotten good grill marks, turn the pitas to the other side and let them cook for another minute or so.

7. Remove the pitas to a sheet pan and spread the sauce over each one.

8. Sprinkle ¼ cup mozzarella over the sauce on each pita . . .

11. Divide the rest of the mozzarella between the pitas . . .

13. Broil the pizzas until the cheese is melted and creamy, 1 to 2 minutes. Sprinkle on the green onion and some pepper flakes and cut into wedges to serve with grated Parmesan on the side.

VARIATIONS

- *Use regular pepperoni slices instead of the large and small combo.*
- *Top the pizza with any combination of ingredients you like!*

9. Then lay on the larger pepperoni . . .

12. And add the mini pepperoni and black olives.

10. And the strips of bell pepper.

Me and my two shadows!

Meaty pizza in minutes!

Burger Central

As much as I love steaks, they are one of the last things I want to order when I travel to different locales. I can cook a good steak at home, after all, and I usually want to experiment with other menu items. However, the same is not true for burgers. I'll order a burger in New York City or Nashville, Oklahoma City or Seattle, just to experience different interpretations on the burger theme. Not to knock chain fast-food joints, as they definitely have their place in our lives from time to time, but I fear they might have contributed to folks forgetting just how exquisite a really good burger can be. So check out (and make!) the burgers in this chapter! Each one is totally different from the one before, and if you've gotten a little *meh* about burgers in recent years, this chapter might awaken the passion again!

Peppery Ranch Dressing
(page 6)

The most flavorful
burger I've ever made!

SURPRISE BURGERS

🕐 30 MINUTES MAKES 2 LARGE STUFFED BURGERS

My mom used to make what she called "surprise burgers" back in the '70s, and while some versions of that recipe called for a burger to be baked within an enclosed bun, hers involved simply enclosing burger fixins (usually ketchup, mustard, and pickles) within the cooked patty itself. Well, since I am a rambunctious child (albeit a fifty-four-year-old one), I can't leave well enough alone, and I like my surprise burger stuffed with all kinds of big-flavor madness. This takes a few steps (none of them complicated), and the result is 100 percent worth it! Maybe 110 percent . . .

2 tablespoons salted butter

4 ounces white or brown button mushrooms, thinly sliced

Steak seasoning, for sprinkling

1 pound ground beef

Kosher salt and ground black pepper

3 tablespoons Caramelized Onions (page 12; see Note, page 235)

6 cloves Garlic Confit (page 3; see Note, page 235)

2 teaspoons whole-grain mustard

FOR SERVING

Peppery Ranch Dressing (page 6)

2 hamburger buns

Crumbled blue cheese

Lettuce leaves

Tomato slices

1. Heat the butter in a large skillet over medium heat. Add the mushrooms and cook, stirring occasionally, until lightly browned, about 4 minutes . . .

3. In a large bowl, season the beef with a generous pinch of salt and pepper, then stir it to soften and mix it up.

5. And add the caramelized onions . . .

2. Then sprinkle on the steak seasoning and continue cooking, stirring occasionally, while you get the meat mixture ready.

4. When the mushrooms are browned, remove them to a bowl . . .

6. The garlic confit cloves . . .

7. And the mustard.

8. Stir to mix it together.

9. Divide the meat mixture in half and form 2 patties that are about 1 inch wider than the buns.

10. Spoon half the mushroom mixture on the middle of one of the patties, leaving a border.

11. Fold the outer edges of the patty in . . .

12. Tucking in the filling as you go . . .

13. Until you can tuck the filling entirely inside the burger. Pinch the edges to help seal.

14. Press and continue to form the burger until it feels tight and secure, then repeat to stuff the other patty!

15. Heat a large cast-iron skillet over medium heat and place the patties in seal side down (just to help lock everything in).

16. Cook the burgers for 6 to 7 minutes per side to ensure the meat is cooked through and the filling is very hot.

17. To serve each burger, spread peppery ranch on both halves of a burger bun.

18. Then place a patty on the bun and pile on crumbled blue cheese.

Note: If you don't have caramelized onions and garlic confit already made, just cook some sliced onion and pressed garlic with the mushrooms until they're all soft and golden.

19. Add lettuce and tomato and *go in*!

Seven hundred years of marriage later, I still feel fizzy when I see him on his horse!

FREDDIE'S BURGER

⏱ 10 MINUTES **MAKES 1 DOUBLE CHEESEBURGER**

Somewhere along the way in the burger universe, a narrative was put forth that super-thick, meaty burgers are the desired way to go. However, take it from me, the wife of a cattle rancher and the maker of burgers for cowboy types: Thin, stacked burgers are far superior! There's more surface area to ensure great flavor, and you can layer a couple of patties with double the cheese, and the whole experience is just . . . well, the way a burger should be. We call this a Freddie's Burger after the yummy burger and ice cream chain in this part of the country, but feel free to call it exactly what it is: a super-thin stacked double cheeseburger!

6 ounces ground beef

Kosher salt and ground black pepper

1 tablespoon butter

1 tablespoon yellow mustard

2 slices American cheese

1 standard-size soft hamburger bun

FOR SERVING (OPTIONAL)

Green leaf lettuce

Dill pickle slices

Thinly sliced white onion

Tomato slices

1. Divide the ground beef in half and flatten each half into a rough round patty. Use your fingers to press and flatten them as much as you can. (They should be about 1 inch larger in diameter than the hamburger bun, since they'll shrink while cooking.)

3. When the skillet has fully heated, melt the butter and swirl it around, then add the patties. Immediately press firmly on each patty with a solid spatula and flatten it a little more on the pan. (Tip: Push the bottom of a metal cup measure against the flat part of the spatula if you need more leverage.)

5. Flip them to the mustard side and press again.

6. Lay the slices of cheese on top and turn the heat to low. Let the cheese melt while the burgers finish cooking, about 1 minute. Hasten the melting by putting the lid (or a sheet pan) on top of the skillet.

2. Season both sides of the patties with a pinch of salt and pepper. Preheat a large cast-iron skillet over medium heat.

4. Squirt a teaspoon or so of mustard on each patty and let them cook for a minute or so, until you see the edges starting to get a little brown underneath.

7. Using the spatula, set one of the patties on the other. (I'll usually put the smaller of the two on top if there's any size difference.)

8. As soon as the cheese looks really melty, place the patties on the bottom bun. Eat the burger as is or top with lettuce, pickles, onion, and tomato.

VARIATIONS

- *For an Oklahoma onion burger, add paper-thin onion slices to the tops of the patties with the mustard. When you flip the burger, the onions will quickly cook!*
- *Substitute pepper Jack or Swiss for American.*
- *Serve the patties on toasted rye bread!*

Ladd's favorite burger, hands down!

CHEESESTEAK BURGER

🕐 25 MINUTES   MAKES 1 HUGE DOUBLE BURGER, TO SERVE 1 OR 2

What a mouthful of marvelousness! Cheesesteaks are a singular sensation, and no matter how many times I've tried, I've never been able to create one as good as the originals in Philly. However, I do make a burger version of a cheesesteak that not only mimics all the flavors and components of the original, it's also huge, tall, gargantuan, mammoth, and ridiculous in the most delicious of ways. Eat this with people who love you for who you are, not for your table manners!

2 tablespoons salted butter

¼ small yellow onion, sliced

¼ small red bell pepper, sliced

4 white mushrooms, sliced

Kosher salt and ground black pepper

2 teaspoons steak seasoning

8 ounces ground beef, formed into 2 patties

Kosher salt and ground black pepper

¼ cup processed cheese sauce, such as Cheez Whiz

2 slices provolone cheese

2 tablespoons spicy mustard

1 sesame seed or other burger bun

1. Heat the butter in a large skillet over medium heat. Add the onion, bell pepper, mushroom, and a pinch of salt and pepper.

3. And cook the vegetables, stirring frequently, until deep golden and soft, about 10 minutes.

5. Season the burgers with the remaining 1 teaspoon steak seasoning and a pinch of salt and pepper, then add them to the pan. Smash the patties a bit thinner with a spatula and let them cook for 4 to 5 minutes on one side.

2. Sprinkle in 1 teaspoon of the steak seasoning . . .

4. Remove them to a plate and set them aside.

6. Meanwhile, in a small saucepan or skillet, heat the cheese sauce over medium-low heat, stirring occasionally, until it's hot.

If a cheesesteak and
a burger got married!

7. Flip the burger patties and add a provolone slice to each. Let the burgers finish cooking for 4 minutes, or until no longer pink, while the cheese melts.

9. Stack one patty on top of the other on the bottom bun . . .

11. And pour on the cheese sauce!

8. To build the burgers, squeeze mustard on the bottom bun.

10. Then pile on as many veggies as you can . . .

Come to Mama!

"They're right behind me, aren't they?"

CHICKEN APPLE SAGE BURGERS

🕐 35 MINUTES **MAKES 2 GENEROUS BURGERS**

Beef burgers are the king, but this chicken burger—with a nice flavor boost from cooked apples and garlic—is an absolute treasure and a downright delightful departure from the original. I first made it in the fall, when fresh sage and apples were all around me—but it's super in the spring, sensational in the summer, and wonderful in the winter as well! Ladd Drummond would never eat this burger, by the way, because it's not made from beef and it's got fruit in it, so I make 'em one at a time for myself. Oh, yes and oh, yum!

1 Granny Smith apple, plus a few apple slices for serving

2 tablespoons olive oil

2 green onions, thinly sliced

3 garlic cloves, minced

1 tablespoon minced fresh sage leaves

Pinch of red pepper flakes

Kosher salt and ground black pepper

1 pound ground chicken

FOR SERVING

Honey Chipotle Crema (page 24) or other zesty creamy sauce

2 brioche burger buns

Bibb lettuce leaves

Tomato slices

Pickled Peppers (page 4)

1. Grate the apple using the large holes of a box grater.

3. Sprinkle in the pepper flakes, as well as a pinch of salt and pepper . . .

2. Heat 1 tablespoon of the olive oil in a large skillet over medium heat and add the apples, green onions, garlic, and sage.

4. Then cook the mixture for about 5 minutes, stirring often, to release the flavors and cook off some of the moisture from the apples. Remove the pan from the heat and let the mixture cool for 5 minutes.

5. Place the chicken in a large bowl and add the apple mixture . . .

6. Then stir to mix thoroughly.

7. Form the mixture into 2 large patties. Note that the mixture is very wet and easier to form than ground beef!

8. In the same skillet, heat the remaining 1 tablespoon olive oil over medium heat and add the burgers.

9. Cook the burgers for 5 minutes on one side, then flip them and cook them for another 6 to 7 minutes, until cooked through. (The internal temperature should be 165°F.)

10. To build a burger, spread the crema on each side of a bun.

11. Place a patty on the bottom bun . . .

12. Then top the burger with lettuce, tomato, and apple slices.

13. Finally, pile on the pickled peppers!

Honey Chipotle Crema
(page 24)

There's apple
in it and on it!

CHEESEBURGER BOWLS

🕐 20 MINUTES **MAKES 4 SERVINGS**

Imagine the best cheeseburger dinner you can think of, with classic toppings, ketchup, and mustard, and onion rings on the side. The meal they serve as you enter the Pearly Gates, in other words. Okay, now picture that whole scenario without the bun. Got that picture? Okay, now picture it served in a nifty bowl, all fancy-like. Cheeseburger bowls are sweeping the nation! Not really, but they should. Let's start with your house and see where this thing goes!

Two 16-ounce packages frozen onion rings

4 pre-formed burger patties (or form your own from ground beef)

1 tablespoon olive oil

2 tablespoons steak seasoning

4 slices cheddar cheese

Ketchup and mustard

1 cup shredded lettuce

1 tomato, diced

Pickle slices

Jarred jalapeño slices

1. Preheat the oven according to the directions on the onion ring bag and a grill pan over medium-high heat.

2. Pour the onion rings onto a sheet pan, then spread them out and get them in the oven.

4. Sprinkle the steak seasoning on the patties . . .

6. And lay slices of cheese on the other side. Cook the patties until no longer pink, another 4 to 5 minutes.

3. Place the patties on a sheet pan and drizzle over the olive oil . . .

5. Then cook the patties on a grill pan (or in a cast-iron skillet) over medium-high heat for 4 to 5 minutes on the first side. Turn them over . . .

7. When the onion rings are golden and the patties are done, it's time to build the bowls!

Hey! Where's the bun?!?

8. Arrange 8 to 10 onion rings in a wide bowl, overlapping and stacking them to make a nice base for the burger.

9. Lay on a burger patty . . .

10. Then drizzle on some ketchup and mustard . . .

11. Sprinkle on the lettuce and tomato . . .

12. And top with the pickles and jalapeños. Repeat to make the rest of the bowls and dive in!

~~~~~~~~~~~~~~~~~~~~~~~~

VARIATIONS

- *Use crinkle-cut French fries instead of onion rings.*

- *Build a bacon ranch cheeseburger by drizzling on ranch instead of ketchup and mustard and topping with crumbled cooked bacon.*

- *Make a Tex-Mex version by substituting pepper Jack cheese for the cheddar and adding guacamole, salsa, and sour cream on top.*

I'd still choose Ladd over Kevin Costner. (But Kevin is second!!)

PATTY MELTS

🕑 20 MINUTES   MAKES 2 SANDWICHES

A patty melt is an absolutely essential part of any burger menu, and sometimes I worry that they are starting to fall off the radar for younger whippersnapper generations, from Gen Z and beyond. I just happen to very firmly believe that in the same way the young people in the world need to know about Simon and Garfunkel, they also need to know about patty melts.

Patty melts are simple: a cooked hamburger patty, caramelized onions, crispy grilled rye bread, Swiss cheese. And this version, which utilizes pre-made caramelized onions, means you can get your patty melt on the table in record time! Ladies and gentlemen (and young people everywhere), I present to you the wonderful, beautiful patty melt . . . also known as my favorite burger on the planet.

1 pound ground beef

4 dashes Worcestershire sauce

Kosher salt and ground black pepper

3 tablespoons butter, plus more as needed

2 mounded tablespoons whole-grain mustard

4 slices rye bread

8 slices Swiss cheese

¼ cup Caramelized Onions (page 12; see Note, page 248), warmed in the microwave for 30 seconds

1. In a medium bowl, combine the ground beef with the Worcestershire.

3. Melt 1 tablespoon of the butter in a large skillet over medium heat and add the patties.

5. Meanwhile, get the sandwiches ready by spreading mustard on 2 slices of bread . . .

2. Add a pinch of salt and pepper and mix to combine. Form the meat into 2 equal-size patties.

4. Cook them until they're no longer pink in the middle, 4 to 5 minutes per side.

6. Then top both slices with overlapping slices of cheese.

7. Spread the onions on each patty and turn off the heat.

8. Place the patties on top of the cheese . . .

9. Then top each patty with another 2 slices of cheese and spread the rest of the mustard on the other 2 bread slices.

10. Put the tops on . . .

11. Then use a couple of paper towels to wipe the excess grease out of the skillet. (Be careful; the skillet is still hot!) Turn the heat to medium-low . . .

12. And when it's ready, add the remaining 2 tablespoons butter and swirl to coat the pan.

13. Grill the patties on one side until the cheese starts to melt on the underside, taking care not to burn the bread (turn down the heat if it starts to brown too fast) . . .

14. Then flip them over and cook until the rest of the cheese is melted and gooey. If the bread seems dry, add a little more butter to the skillet.

15. Remove the patty melts from the pan and slice them in half with a serrated knife.

Yep. The world definitely needs more patty melts!

Note: If you do not have jarred caramelized onions, make them in the skillet before you cook the burgers: Thinly slice half a yellow onion. Melt 2 tablespoons of butter over medium heat, add the onion, and cook, stirring often, until the onion is soft and caramelized, 15 to 18 minutes.

My #1 burger
of choice!

Caramelized Onions
(page 12)

Expecting Company

❀

Does anyone have guests for dinner anymore? Sometimes I wonder if the past few years of busyness and upheaval have turned us more inward, and when we do have a Friday or Saturday night with nothing to do, we either grab a bite in a restaurant or stay home and have lazy downtime in faded black yoga pants watching really high-quality reality television while eating blue corn chips with salsa verde and handfuls of chocolate chips and a glass of wine. (Okay, that got a little specific, Ree!) Point is, let's start having buddies over for dinner! It doesn't have to be fancy, your house doesn't have to look perfect, and by golly, the memories last forever!

A stupendous
snacking supper!

ANTIPASTO SNACKING SUPPER

🕐 15 MINUTES MAKES 4 TO 6 SERVINGS

I know charcuterie, antipasto, and any sort of cheese-and-crackers situation tend to serve as a little bite before a larger meal, but I love that category of food so much that I often wonder why it doesn't count as the meal itself. Especially in the sweaty summertime, nothing makes a more perfect dinner to me than this beautiful array of meats, cheeses, and jarred goodies—and the little wedges of grilled bread on the side make the whole thing seem complete! (Correction: The glass of chilled white wine makes the whole thing seem complete! As glasses of chilled white wine tend to do.) You will love this supper of snacks!

6 tablespoons (¾ stick) salted butter, at room temperature

2 garlic cloves, pressed

3 ciabatta rolls, split

3 tablespoons extra-virgin olive oil

2 tablespoons balsamic vinegar

1 tablespoon balsamic glaze, plus more for serving

½ teaspoon dried oregano

Kosher salt and ground black pepper

2 romaine hearts, chopped

A few salami slices, cut into strips

A few thin soppressata slices

A few thin prosciutto slices

¼ cup sliced roasted red peppers

½ cup grape tomatoes, halved

½ cup marinated quartered artichoke hearts

½ cup marinated olives

1 cup mozzarella balls (bocconcini)

1. Preheat a grill pan over medium-low heat.

2. Mash the butter with half the pressed garlic, mixing thoroughly.

4. Place the rolls butter side down on the grill pan . . .

3. Smear all the cut ciabatta sides with the garlic butter.

5. And turn them over when good grill marks form. Turn the heat to low and slowly grill the other side while you make the dressing.

6. In a jar, combine the olive oil, balsamic vinegar, balsamic glaze, remaining pressed garlic, and the oregano. Sprinkle in a pinch of salt and pepper.

7. Screw on the lid and shake until thoroughly mixed.

8. Remove the bread and cut each piece into 4 wedges.

9. Place the lettuce in a large bowl and drizzle on half of the dressing . . .

10. Toss, then pour the lettuce onto a large platter. Drizzle with the rest of the dressing to taste.

11. Arrange the meats, roasted peppers, tomatoes, artichoke hearts, olives, and mozzarella in piles on top of the lettuce. Drizzle the balsamic glaze over the mozzarella and serve with the bread on the side.

~~~~~~~~~~~~~~~~~~~

TIPS

- *For individual portions, build beautiful arrangements in pasta bowls.*
- *Dump any leftovers into a sealable plastic bag and make a sandwich with it the next day!*

My favorite person to eat with!

CRAB CAKES WITH RÉMOULADE

⏱ 20 MINUTES MAKES 8 LARGE CRAB CAKES, TO SERVE 4

A good crab cake is so, so good, and I love that you can decide what they are depending on the occasion. Have a favorite friend dropping by for a drink? Make them to enjoy as a snack with wine. Having ladies over for lunch? Serve them with a pretty arugula salad. Wanting to rock the surf and turf for your nuclear family to celebrate how much you love 'em? Whip these up to serve with grilled steak. These cook under the broiler, which makes them blissfully mess-free. Zero reasons not to make these soon!

1 large egg

1¼ cups mayonnaise

2 tablespoons chopped fresh parsley, plus more for serving

1½ teaspoons Old Bay seasoning

½ teaspoon garlic salt

1 teaspoon Dijon mustard

Grated zest and juice of 1 lemon

Kosher salt and ground black pepper

½ cup panko breadcrumbs

1 pound lump crabmeat, fresh or canned

4 tablespoons (½ stick) butter, melted

1 tablespoon capers, drained and chopped

Lemon wedges, for serving

1. Position a rack in the middle of the oven and preheat the broiler.

2. In a large bowl, combine the egg, ½ cup of the mayonnaise, the parsley, Old Bay, garlic salt, mustard, lemon zest, and a pinch of salt and pepper.

3. Stir until everything is mixed.

4. Add the panko and crabmeat . . .

5. And fold the mixture until everything is combined.

6. Brush a sheet pan with some of the melted butter.

7. Use a ⅓-cup measure to remove portions of the crab mixture from the bowl.

8. Pat them into neat discs and place them on the pan.

9. Brush the tops with melted butter and set the sheet pan on the middle oven rack. Broil the crab cakes until the tops are golden and crisp, 5 to 7 minutes.

The brothers who work cattle together, stay together.

10. Make the rémoulade by mixing the remaining 1 cup mayonnaise with the lemon juice, capers, and a pinch of salt and pepper in a medium bowl.

11. Remove the crab cakes and serve them with the rémoulade, a sprinkle of parsley, and lemon wedges.

Serve as an appetizer, a side, or a main dish!

ITALIAN OVEN MEATBALLS

🕐 30 MINUTES **MAKES 6 TO 8 SERVINGS**

I spent years and years on a hamster wheel of frying meatballs anytime I made them, whether they were for spaghetti, subs, or appetizers. I don't know how I got into that groove, but over the past year I've unleashed the power of the oven when it comes to my meatball-making life, and I'm not sure I'll go back to the frying method. I am an impatient home cook, after all, and if I can figure out a way to slap things on a pan, hurl them into the oven, and have a few extra minutes of freedom, I'm gonna jump on it! This is now my go-to meatball recipe, and I love to either simmer them in marinara after they're cooked, or serve them on a beautiful platter of greens. Meatballs and me . . . I think we have a very bright future together!

1 pound ground pork

1 pound Italian sausage, casings removed

½ cup grated mozzarella cheese

¼ cup grated Parmesan cheese

½ cup prepared pesto

2 tablespoons balsamic glaze, plus more for dressing the salad and drizzling

½ teaspoon red pepper flakes

Kosher salt and ground black pepper

4 to 5 cups packed baby arugula

2 tablespoons olive oil

1 cup halved yellow cherry tomatoes

½ cup sliced jarred roasted peppers

Parmesan shavings, for serving

1. Position a rack in the middle of the oven and preheat the broiler. Line a sheet pan with foil.

2. In a large bowl, combine the ground pork, sausage, mozzarella, and Parmesan.

3. Add the pesto, balsamic glaze, pepper flakes, and a pinch of salt and pepper.

4. Stir and mix everything thoroughly.

No more frying meatballs for me!

5. Use a ¼-cup scoop or measure to form meatballs and set them on the lined pan.

8. Place the tomatoes and roasted red peppers on the arugula . . .

9. And arrange the meatballs all over the top and add shaved Parmesan. Drizzle with balsamic glaze!

6. Set the pan on the middle oven rack and broil the meatballs until they are browned and cooked through, 15 to 17 minutes.

7. Arrange the arugula on a platter and drizzle with the olive oil and a little balsamic glaze.

There's that dang smile again!

Fancy Fried Fish

⏱ **45 MINUTES**   **MAKES 6 SERVINGS**

Holy *mackerel*! Ha ha, sorry. Had to get that out of the way. I mean holy *cod*! This very simple beer-battered fried fish, with the addition of lovely zucchini sticks, is truly a delicious delight. It has all the comfort food goodness of a certain fried fish fast-food chain that we fell in love with in the 1980s but with a lovely, light, batter that's unmistakably homemade.

Have all the elements prepped before you get started, because you'll want to serve it very freshly fried!

Vegetable oil, for deep-frying

2 cups all-purpose flour

2 teaspoons kosher salt

2 teaspoons ground black pepper

2 teaspoons baking powder

¼ cup cornstarch

One 12-ounce bottle brown ale or beer

2 medium zucchini (1 pound total), cut into 3 × ½-inch batons

1½ pounds cod or haddock fillets, cut into ¾-inch strips

Store-bought tartar sauce

Lemon wedges, for serving

Fresh parsley leaves, for serving

1. Pour a few inches of vegetable oil into a large Dutch oven and heat it over medium-high heat until it reaches 375°F on an oil/candy thermometer. Set a wire rack over a sheet pan and set aside.

2. Set up the assembly line for breading: In one baking dish, combine ½ cup of the flour and 1 teaspoon each of the salt and pepper.

3. In the second dish, combine the remaining 1½ cups flour, the remaining 1 teaspoon each salt and pepper, the baking powder, and cornstarch.

4. Whisk each mixture to combine.

5. Slowly pour the ale into the dish with the cornstarch, gently whisking as you pour. Keep whisking until the mixture resembles pancake batter.

6. Start breading the zucchini by dropping a few pieces at a time in the dry mix. Toss to coat, then shake off the excess . . .

7. And dunk them in the batter. Let the excess drip off . . .

8. Then slowly drop them in the hot oil.

9. Use a spider or slotted metal spoon to move the zucchini around the oil as they cook.

10. Remove the zucchini when the breading is beautifully golden, 3 to 4 minutes, and set them on the wire rack to drain. Continue to fry the rest of the zucchini . . .

11. Then bread the fish the same way . . .

12. And fry it in batches.

13. Let the fish fry until the breading is golden, 3 to 4 minutes, then let it drain with the zucchini.

14. Keep going until everything is fried . . .

15. Then serve the fish and zucchini fries with tartar sauce, lemon wedges, and a sprinkle of parsley.

Fried fish has never
been more fabulous!

STICKY BBQ-GLAZED PORK TENDERLOIN

🕐 40 MINUTES MAKES 4 TO 6 SERVINGS

I don't care what anyone says (nice attitude, Ree!): Pork tenderloin is boring. Well, wait a sec . . . correction: Pork tenderloin is boring unless you jazz it up and have a blast with it, which is exactly what happens with this yummy, colorful, and delightfully messy dinner! It is gloriously saucy, with a cool and spicy fruit relish, and if you serve this to friends, they will tell all *their* friends about it. And then you'll have more friends than you know what to do with! Enter at your own risk.

2 tablespoons smoked paprika

1 tablespoon packed brown sugar

1 teaspoon garlic powder

1 teaspoon onion powder

1 teaspoon kosher salt

1 teaspoon ground black pepper

2 whole pork tenderloins (about 1 pound each)

2 tablespoons olive oil

1 cup of your favorite barbecue sauce

PINEAPPLE SALSA

1 cup diced pineapple (fresh or canned is fine!)

3 jalapeños, seeded and finely diced

1 poblano pepper, seeded and finely diced

1 large red bell pepper, diced

¼ cup chopped fresh cilantro

Kosher salt and ground black pepper

Juice of 2 limes

1. Preheat the oven to 400°F.

2. In a small bowl, mix together the smoked paprika, brown sugar, garlic powder, onion powder, salt, and pepper.

3. Lay the tenderloins on a sheet pan and sprinkle the seasoning mix on all sides. Rub it in a bit and let them sit while you heat a large cast-iron skillet over medium-high heat.

4. Pour the olive oil into the preheated pan and lay the tenderloins in the oil.

5. Sear the tenderloins on all sides until nicely browned, about 5 minutes total.

Page 312!

Sticky, sweet, and sensational!

6. Brush on half the barbecue sauce, transfer the pan to the oven, and roast until the outside is nicely browned, about 10 minutes.

7. Remove the pan and pour the other half of the sauce over the tenderloins. Roast until the pork is done in the center, 6 to 8 minutes more. If you like a little more blackened surface, broil them for 3 to 4 minutes to deepen the color.

8. Remove the tenderloins from the oven and set the pan aside.

9. Make the pineapple salsa: In a large bowl, combine the pineapple, jalapeños, poblano, bell pepper, cilantro, and a pinch of salt and pepper. Squeeze in the lime juice . . .

"Hey, Mom . . . is it lunchtime yet?"

10. And stir to mix everything.

11. Serve the tenderloins on a platter with the salsa piled on top. (Slice them first if you like—whatever your preference!)

GARLIC HERB LAMB CHOPS

⏱ 20 MINUTES MAKES 4 SERVINGS

We don't eat a lot of lamb in Oklahoma given that it's cattle country around here, but every time I do enjoy a lamb chop dinner, I wonder why we don't work it into our rotation more often. For those who don't ever cook lamb themselves, one might assume it's difficult to make, but these little rib chops are even easier to cook than steak! They're nice and small, they always look elegant, and I love to make them for my slightly fancy friends. (And okay, my slightly fancy self.)

2 teaspoons kosher salt

1 teaspoon ground black pepper

3 garlic cloves, minced

Leaves from 1 fresh rosemary sprig, minced

½ teaspoon red pepper flakes

Grated zest of 1 lemon

One 2-pound 8-rib rack of lamb

¼ cup olive oil

Pimento Cheese Grits (page 314) or mashed potatoes, for serving

1. In a small bowl, combine the salt, pepper, garlic, rosemary, pepper flakes, and lemon zest . . .

3. Cut the rack of lamb into individual chops by holding the bone and slicing down between the bones.

5. And thoroughly rub it onto the surface. Turn the chops over and season the other side with the rest of the seasoning.

2. And stir with a fork until everything is mixed.

4. Sprinkle half of the seasoning on one side of the chops . . .

6. Heat the olive oil in a large cast-iron skillet over medium-high heat. Cook for 3 minutes on one side, moving the chops around a bit as they cook.

7. Then turn them over and cook them for about 2 minutes on the second side, until medium to medium-rare.

8. Remove the chops to a plate and let them rest for 5 minutes.

9. Serve the chops on grits or mashed potatoes.

Built Paige tough!

Pimento Cheese Grits (page 314)!

You will love these lamb chops!

Thin breakfast chops
are the star of this show!

FIVE-SPICE PORK CHOP BOWLS

⏱ 15 MINUTES MAKES 2 TO 4 BOWLS

I usually cook thin breakfast pork chops for Ladd and Todd. It's their favorite food, and they love them breaded and fried—a lot like chicken-fried steak. But thin pork chops are truly one of the world's best cuts of meat, and you can take them in any flavor direction you like. I love to use them in these beautiful, bountiful rice bowls. Five-spice powder makes them marvelous!

4 thin-cut bone-in pork chops (known as breakfast chops)

Olive oil, for brushing and drizzling

Kosher salt and ground black pepper

A few pinches Chinese five-spice powder

2 heads baby bok choy

1 large red bell pepper, cut into large chunks

FOR THE BOWLS

1 cup jasmine rice, cooked according to the package directions

2 tablespoons hoisin sauce

2 tablespoons sriracha

2 green onions, thinly sliced

1. Put the pork chops on a sheet pan and brush both sides with some olive oil, then sprinkle all over with pinches of salt, pepper, and five-spice powder.

3. While the chops are cooking, slice the bok choy in half lengthwise.

5. Turn the chops over and cook them for another 2 minutes, pressing them to flatten.

2. Preheat a grill pan or iron skillet over medium-high heat. Cook the pork chops for 3 to 4 minutes on one side.

4. Drizzle them with a little olive oil and sprinkle with a little salt, pepper, and five-spice powder.

6. Remove the chops to a plate and set them aside to rest.

7. Place the bok choy (cut side down) and red pepper chunks on the grill and let them cook for 4 minutes on one side.

8. Turn them over and let them cook until slightly tender, another 3 minutes.

9. Scoop one-quarter of the cooked rice into a wide bowl and add a pork chop.

10. Arrange a bok choy half and chunks of red bell pepper in the bowl . . .

11. Then add a drizzle of hoisin . . .

12. Some sriracha . . .

13. And a sprinkle of green onions!

This vacation photo is sponsored by the color blue.

SEAFOOD CASSEROLE FROM THE '70S

🕐 45 MINUTES **MAKES 6 TO 8 SERVINGS**

The recipes I remember my mom making in the '70s and '80s, when there seemed to be a never-ending calendar of dinner parties and luncheons going on, will never, ever leave my food memory. I can still taste all the salads, the soufflés, and the casseroles—specifically this incredibly indulgent medley of shellfish baked in a creamy wine "sauce." When you see what the main ingredient is in the sauce, you will chuckle. It's all a little bit wacky . . . but somehow, it all makes scrumptious sense!

2 cups mayonnaise

2 tablespoons Dijon mustard

3 tablespoons sherry wine

3 dashes of Worcestershire sauce

Hot sauce

1 teaspoon Old Bay seasoning

Kosher salt and ground black pepper

1 cup lump crabmeat (fresh, frozen, or canned)

1 cup chopped cooked shrimp

1 cup lump cooked lobster meat

1 cup finely diced celery

1 small green bell pepper, finely diced

4 green onions, thinly sliced

3 cups kettle-cooked or regular potato chips

2 tablespoons chopped fresh flat-leaf parsley

1. Preheat the oven to 375°F.

2. In a large bowl, combine the mayonnaise, mustard, sherry, Worcestershire, hot sauce, Old Bay, and a pinch of salt and pepper . . .

4. Dump in *allllll* the seafood. What a glorious sight!

3. Stir until smooth, then taste and adjust the seasonings. (Sometimes I add a touch more sherry!)

5. Add the celery, bell pepper, and green onions . . .

An easy, elegant
'70s marvel!

6. And mix everything together.

7. Pour the mixture into a 3-quart baking dish and spread it out evenly. Crush the potato chips in a plastic bag. You'll want a mix of smaller bits and larger chunks.

8. Sprinkle the chips over the top. Slide the casserole into the oven and bake the casserole for 30 minutes . . .

9. Until the chips are golden and the seafood mixture is slightly bubbling.

10. Sprinkle on the parsley and serve!

VARIATIONS

- After stirring the seafood mixture together, cover the bowl and chill it for a couple of hours. Serve it as a seafood salad on lettuce leaves!

- Spoon the seafood salad into a soft bun to make a play on a lobster roll.

- Omit the lobster and bulk up the crab and shrimp for a less expensive casserole!

This laundry was *not* a part of our wedding vows.

PORK MARSALA WITH MUSHROOMS

🕐 35 MINUTES MAKES 3 TO 6 SERVINGS

This supper is basically my weakness. First, I love noodles. Second, I am obsessed with mushrooms. Third, and possibly most relevant, I am powerless around any creamy wine sauce. Throw those three factors together and it explains why this dish makes my knees turn to spaghetti! (Or egg noodles in this case!) Chicken Marsala is a classic, but I love to switch in pork chops whenever I have 'em in my fridge. You'll love this elegant dish for company!

6 thin boneless pork chops (about ½ inch thick)

Kosher salt and ground black pepper

½ cup all-purpose flour

2 tablespoons olive oil

8 tablespoons (1 stick) salted butter

1 pound white button mushrooms, quartered

1 cup Marsala wine

1 cup low-sodium beef broth, plus more as needed

2 teaspoons cornstarch

½ cup heavy cream

3 or 4 dashes of Worcestershire sauce

12 ounces egg noodles, cooked according to the package directions, drained, and kept warm

Grated zest of 1 lemon

¼ cup minced fresh flat-leaf parsley, plus more for garnish

1. A couple at a time, place the pork chops between two pieces of plastic wrap and pound them with the flat side of a mallet to ¼ inch thick.

3. In a shallow dish, season the flour with a generous pinch of salt and pepper and stir to combine, then add the pork chops, two at a time . . .

5. Shake off the excess flour and set the pork chops on a plate. Repeat to coat the rest of the chops.

2. Sprinkle both sides with a pinch of salt and pepper.

4. And turn them over to coat both sides in the seasoned flour.

6. Heat 1 tablespoon of the olive oil and 2 tablespoons of the butter in a large skillet over medium-high heat. Add three of the pork chops and cook for 3 minutes . . .

Ticks all the yummy
boxes for me!

7. Then flip them and let them cook until no longer pink, another 3 minutes. Remove them to a plate.

8. Add the remaining 1 tablespoon olive oil and 2 more tablespoons of the butter and cook the rest of the pork chops. Set them aside to rest.

9. Add the mushrooms to the pan, stirring them around to let them soak up all the flavor. Cook them, stirring frequently, for 5 to 6 minutes.

10. Add the Marsala, then stir, scraping up the flavorful bits from the bottom of the pan.

11. Add the broth . . .

12. And cook the mushrooms in the liquid, stirring often and letting it reduce by half, 3 to 4 minutes.

13. Reduce the heat to medium-low. In a small pitcher, whisk the cornstarch and heavy cream together, then pour the mixture into the sauce.

14. Add the Worcestershire and stir, then let it bubble and thicken for about 1 minute. Turn off the heat.

15. Melt the remaining 4 tablespoons butter in a small pan and drizzle it over the noodles in a large bowl.

16. Add the lemon zest, parsley, and a pinch of salt and pepper.

17. Stir to totally coat the noodles.

18. Place some noodles on a large plate and add one or two pork chops. Spoon the mushrooms and sauce all over the pork. Garnish with parsley and serve immediately.

MEATLOAF PATTIES

⏱ **40 MINUTES** **MAKES 4 SERVINGS**

I don't need to tell you how much I love meatloaf, because I have waxed rhapsodic about the stuff since I first started food blogging in 2006. And while it is perfect on its own, I'm very rarely content to leave it alone: I make regular meatloaf, Italian meatloaf, meatloaf muffins, meatloaf pizza. Give me time and I'm sure I'll find some way to turn meatloaf into dessert of some sort. Never mind; no I won't. Meatloaf should definitely live forever in the savory category!

One brilliant way to get meatloaf on the table faster than normal is to make it into individual patties! And because wrapping patties in bacon can be a little clunky, I love to do a proud crisscross presentation on top and serve the whole thing on mashed potatoes. Divine!

8 slices bacon

½ yellow onion

1½ pounds ground chuck

¼ cup plain breadcrumbs

¼ cup chopped fresh flat-leaf parsley

4 garlic cloves, grated

1 large egg

¼ cup milk

Kosher salt and ground black pepper

⅓ cup ketchup

1 tablespoon packed brown sugar

½ tablespoon prepared yellow mustard

½ tablespoon hot sauce

1. Preheat the broiler and line a sheet pan with foil.

2. In a large skillet over medium heat, start cooking the bacon. Grate the onion using the large holes on a box grater.

3. In a large bowl, combine the ground chuck, breadcrumbs, parsley, garlic, and egg. Add the grated onion . . .

4. And the milk. Sprinkle in a generous pinch of salt and pepper and mash everything together with your hands or a wooden spoon. Divide the mixture into four equal portions and form them into patties.

Instant Cheesy Mash
(page 311)

Meatloaf can be elegant!

5. Remove the bacon to a paper towel and drain off all but ¼ cup of the grease from the skillet. Reduce the heat to medium-low.

7. Meanwhile, in a small bowl, stir together the ketchup, brown sugar, mustard, and hot sauce.

9. Place the patties on the prepared sheet pan and top with the sauce, spreading to cover them.

6. Lay the patties in the skillet and cook them for 5 to 6 minutes on one side.

8. Flip the patties and cook them until they're no longer pink, another 5 to 6 minutes.

10. Broil on the lowest rack for 8 to 10 minutes, to set the sauce and further roast the outside of the meatloaf patties. Serve each patty with 2 pieces of bacon on top.

Serenity, thy name is Sunrise.

MEDITERRANEAN BAKED TILAPIA

 25 MINUTES **MAKES 4 TO 6 SERVINGS**

I'm married to a cattle rancher (have I ever mentioned that before?), so feasting on fish just hasn't been a practice of mine over the past twenty-five years. But I have been on an absolute fish-feasting jag lately, with no signs of slowing! For a while I was trying to figure out some nutritional or psychological cause of this, but I finally came up with the actual reason: I'm an empty nester now, and I can cook and eat whatever I want!

This absolutely delightful tilapia dinner is Mediterranean-inspired and company-worthy, and it takes less than thirty minutes start to finish. (Fish cooks fast . . . maybe that's another reason I love it lately.)

1 tablespoon chopped fresh rosemary leaves

1 tablespoon chopped fresh oregano

2 teaspoons ground cumin

1 teaspoon ground coriander

1 teaspoon paprika

2 teaspoons kosher salt

1 teaspoon ground black pepper

6 large skinless tilapia fillets

2 tablespoons olive oil

1 cucumber, finely diced

1 cup multicolor cherry tomatoes, halved

½ cup diced pitted kalamata or assorted olives

3 tablespoons chopped fresh flat-leaf parsley

4 tablespoons Zippy Vinaigrette (page 9) or bottled vinaigrette

3 to 4 cups baby arugula

2 bags microwaveable whole grains (in the rice aisle) or your choice of cooked rice

Crumbled feta cheese, for serving

Chopped fresh dill, for serving

1. Preheat the oven to 375°F.

2. In a small bowl, combine the rosemary, oregano, cumin, coriander . . .

3. Paprika, salt, and pepper. Stir to make the seasoning mix.

4. Line a sheet pan with parchment and lay the tilapia on top. Drizzle with the olive oil . . .

5. And sprinkle generously with the seasoning mix. Turn the fillets over and season the other side, then bake the fillets for 12 to 14 minutes.

6. While the fish is baking, make the topping: In a large bowl, combine the cucumber, tomatoes, olives, and parsley. Drizzle in 3 tablespoons of the vinaigrette . . .

10. Remove the fish from the oven when it is light golden and opaque but not dry.

14. Add the feta and dill, then dive into this downright beautiful dinner!

7. And toss to combine.

11. Heat the grains according to the package directions, add a pile to each bowl . . .

Marital mountain hikes: Proceed with caution! (I wasn't smiling by the end.)

8. In a medium bowl, combine the arugula with the remaining 1 tablespoon vinaigrette . . .

12. And place a fillet on top.

9. And toss to coat.

13. Serve the arugula on the side and add a generous spoonful of topping to the fish.

PEPPER BEEF STIR-FRY

⏱ 40 MINUTES **MAKES 4 SERVINGS**

There's nothing faster than a standard stir-fry, and I love just throwing veggies and a protein into a hot wok and turning it into something magical. But every now and then I add a breading step and make this super-duper beef stir-fry, which boasts incredibly crispy strips of fried rib eye tossed in sauce. It is spectacular, and while there are a few steps, if you get everything prepped and laid out ahead of time, the kingdom of flavor heaven is yours!

2 pounds rib eye, sliced into thin strips

2 tablespoons soy sauce

1 teaspoon toasted sesame oil

1 large egg

1 tablespoon ground ginger

Vegetable oil, for frying

½ cup cornstarch

½ cup all-purpose flour

2 tablespoons olive oil

2 tablespoons butter

4 garlic cloves, minced

1 yellow onion, thinly sliced

1 red bell pepper, thinly sliced

1 green bell pepper, thinly sliced

1 cup bottled teriyaki sauce

Sliced green onion, for garnish

Sesame seeds, for garnish

1. Place the rib-eye strips in a large bowl. (Hint: Placing the steaks in the freezer for 20 to 30 minutes makes them easier to slice!)

2. Add the soy sauce . . .

3. And the sesame oil.

4. Crack in the egg . . .

5. And add the ground ginger.

6. Stir to coat the meat well. Heat 1 to 2 inches of vegetable oil in a medium pot over medium heat.

7. Mix the flour and cornstarch in a medium bowl and drop in several rib-eye strips.

8. Toss them around the mixture to coat, then pick them up with tongs and shake off the excess.

9. Drop them into the oil . . .

10. And cook until the breading is crisp, 2 to 3 minutes. Transfer the rib-eye strips to a paper towel–lined tray. Keep frying the beef in batches until done.

11. Heat the olive oil and butter in a wok or large cast-iron skillet over medium-high heat. Add the garlic, onion, and bell peppers . . .

12. And cook, stirring and tossing, until tender and golden, 4 to 5 minutes.

13. Pour in the teriyaki sauce . . .

14. Then add the beef.

15. Stir and toss until the beef and veggies are totally coated in sauce. (There should be no more of the sauce left in the bottom of the pan.)

16. Serve the stir-fry immediately in bowls . . .

17. And sprinkle on green onion and sesame seeds.

VARIATIONS

- *Add different veggies with the garlic and onion: zucchini, mushrooms, summer squash, or eggplant.*
- *Make this a spicy dish by adding dried red chiles or 1 teaspoon red pepper flakes with the onion and bell peppers.*

The crispy strips of
rib eye are magical!

Spiffy Sides

I remember when I used to go out to cafeteria restaurants with my grand-mother Ga-Ga. I'd walk through the seemingly endless food line, marvel at all the individually dished-up choices, and wind up selecting approximately eight different sides (plus Jell-O salad—I never could decide whether that was con-sidered a side or a dessert). I wouldn't even bother with the entrées, because the sides were such an exciting mix of veggies and starches and flavors, I didn't want to complicate things. The collection of sides in this chapter reflect the smorgasbord I enjoyed with Ga-Ga all those years ago! They're easy to whip up, they go with a lot of different main courses, and you can skip the entrée and eat eight of them for dinner if you feel like it!

CRISPY PARMESAN POTATOES

 40 MINUTES **MAKES 4 TO 6 SERVINGS**

For eons, home cooks have tried to crack the code on crispy roasted potatoes—at least this home cook has. So often if you cook them in a skillet, they get shriveled and greasy. If you roast them in the oven, they steam and turn to mush. After twenty-seven years of being domestic, just when I was about to give up and serve frozen fries the rest of my life, I came upon the viral social media method that inspired this tutorial. The prep takes a little patience, and the wait time after roasting takes a lot of patience (because the potatoes smell so good!), but the result is a fantastically tasty potato side that you'll want in your permanent rotation!

1 pound baby potatoes, halved lengthwise	1 teaspoon minced garlic	Kosher salt and ground black pepper
4 tablespoons (½ stick) butter, melted	1 teaspoon minced fresh rosemary leaves	⅓ cup finely grated Parmesan cheese
	1 teaspoon red pepper flakes	

1. Preheat the oven to 450°F.

2. Using a sharp paring knife, carefully score the cut side of each potato half. This helps the crispy cheese mixture adhere to the potatoes after baking!

3. Pour the melted butter onto a sheet pan . . .

4. And add the garlic, rosemary, pepper flakes, and a pinch of salt and pepper.

5. Add the Parmesan . . .

6. And stir to mix, spreading the mixture evenly over the pan.

7. Add the potato halves, cut side down, smearing them into the butter mixture to coat each half. Bake for 25 minutes . . .

Page 271!

So flavorful
and crisp!

~~~~~~~~~~~~~~~~~~~~~~

SERVE WITH

• *A juicy steak or burgers*

• *Grilled chicken or fish*

• *Peppery Ranch Dressing
(page 6) as a dipping sauce!*

8. Until the potatoes are golden and the cheese has started to brown. Set the pan aside and leave the potatoes undisturbed for 8 to 10 minutes to give the cheese a chance to stick.

9. Lift one up to test; if the cheese stays, serve away! If it doesn't, wait another couple of minutes and try again.

My youngest with my oldest!

BALSAMIC BRUSSELS SPROUTS

⏱ 15 MINUTES   **MAKES 2 TO 4 SERVINGS**

These unimaginably tasty sprouts have all the appearance of having been roasted in a blazing hot oven, but they are, quite refreshingly, browned to perfection right in a nonstick skillet. If you've ever been frustrated by waiting for Brussels sprouts to roast and roast and roast, I think you're about to get really excited. These are incredible!

3 tablespoons butter

1 tablespoon olive oil

1 pound Brussels sprouts, trimmed and halved

Kosher salt

2 garlic cloves, minced

1 green onion, thinly sliced, dark green parts separated

1 tablespoon balsamic vinegar

1. In a large nonstick skillet over medium-high heat, melt 2 tablespoons of the butter with the olive oil. Add the Brussels sprouts cut side down . . .

3. Carefully remove the lid. (There'll be a lot of steam!)

5. Turn the heat to low and add the garlic, the whites and light-green parts of the green onion, and a pinch of salt.

2. Then place the lid on the pan and cook, undisturbed, for 5 minutes. This will help the sprouts steam and start to get tender, and it'll really crisp up the bottoms!

4. Grab a fork and check the bottom of one of the sprouts. If they aren't quite brown yet, let them cook for another 2 minutes over medium-high.

6. Stir and cook for another 2 minutes.

Sprouts made in a skillet!

7. Add the balsamic . . .

8. And the remaining 1 tablespoon butter.

9. Toss until a very light sauce coats the sprouts. Serve immediately!

The whole fam at Christmas church!

The ranch work is the same yesterday, today, and tomorrow!
It's nice that some things never change.

PAN-CHARRED BROCCOLI

🕐 15 MINUTES **MAKES 2 SERVINGS**

This super-fast broccoli side is made in the same way as my favorite Brussels sprouts (page 293), and forever made me a believer in the power of char on vegetables. I tend to find broccoli slightly boring from time to time, and this is totally the fix for that. So tasty!

2 heaping cups broccoli florets

4 tablespoons (½ stick) butter

1 tablespoon olive oil

2 garlic cloves, minced

Kosher salt and ground black pepper

Pinch of red pepper flakes

1. Slice the broccoli florets in half lengthwise.

2. Heat 2 tablespoons of the butter and the olive oil in a large skillet over medium-high heat. When the butter is starting to brown, lay the pieces of broccoli in the pan, cut side down.

3. Put the lid on the pan and let the broccoli cook, undisturbed, for 5 minutes.

WHY DOES BROWNED FOOD TASTE SO GOOD?

Whether it's this charred broccoli or the surface of a juicy seared steak, there's nothing more pleasing than food that's been beautifully browned. Whenever you see food that's become brown during cooking or baking, that means the *Maillard reaction* (a chemical reaction between amino acids and sugars) has occurred. Even the deep brown surface of baked bread has the Maillard reaction to thank! It actually alters and transforms the flavor of food (much like salt does!), so don't be afraid to get a good sear on some of your favorite meats and veggies.

Nothing boring about this broccoli!

4. Carefully lift the lid . . .

5. And add the garlic . . .

6. The remaining 2 tablespoons butter, and a pinch of salt and pepper.

7. Stir until the butter is melted, then add the pepper flakes. Stir and serve immediately!

Time for another Basset ear scratch!

ROSEMARY-GARLIC BUTTER BATH BISCUITS

🕐 40 MINUTES **MAKES 9 LARGE BISCUITS**

Here's another social media sensation that's worthy of working into your dinner roll (or breakfast bread) rotation! There are just some things in the universe that simply make sense, and baking biscuits in a literal pool of melted butter is one of them. Goodness, goodness, goodness. (Correction: I mean greatness.) The craggy texture on the tops of the biscuits is otherworldly!

1 cup (2 sticks) butter, melted

4 garlic cloves, minced

Leaves from 1 rosemary sprig, minced

3 cups self-rising flour, plus more for cutting the biscuits

¾ teaspoon kosher salt

2½ cups buttermilk

1 tablespoon minced fresh chives

1. Preheat the oven to 450°F.

2. Melt the butter in a small skillet and add the garlic . . .

4. And stir to mix well. Turn off the heat and set it aside to stay warm in the pan.

6. Pour in the buttermilk, stirring as you go . . .

3. And the rosemary . . .

5. In a large bowl, stir together the self-rising flour and salt.

7. Until everything is incorporated. Note that the batter is very sticky!

8. Pour the butter into a 3-quart baking dish . . .

9. And yes! Scrape the biscuit dough right in.

10. Gently push the dough out to the edges. You'll see the butter coming up around the outside!

11. Flour the blade of a bench scraper or spatula and score two lines evenly spaced the long way (cutting the dough into thirds) and two cuts the short way. You'll wind up with 9 biscuits!

12. Bake the biscuits until the top is very golden, 28 to 30 minutes. Let the dish sit for 5 minutes . . .

13. Then sprinkle on the chives! Serve warm.

VARIATIONS

- Sprinkle the biscuit dough with ¼ cup grated Parmesan before baking.
- Omit the garlic, rosemary, and chives for plain biscuits. (Great for breakfast!)

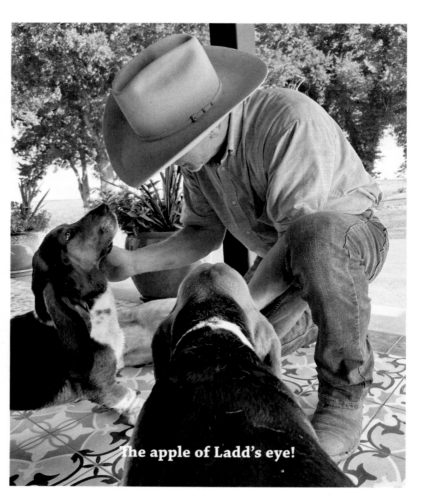

The apple of Ladd's eye!

Biscuits baked in a
bath of butter!

If you've never eaten hominy,
this will win you over!

HOMINY CASSEROLE

45 MINUTES **MAKES 6 TO 8 SERVINGS**

I was torn about whether to include this in the sides chapter, because it's a casserole that could totally pass as a main course if it needed to! Hominy, in case you aren't familiar, is corn that's been treated in a way that makes it plump and pleasantly chewy, and the flavor is very mild and lovely. It isn't a widely used ingredient across America these days, and if I'm being honest, it's not necessarily widely used in Oklahoma—at least as much as it used to be. But oh, is it ever delicious, and this is the best gateway dish to lead others into the hominy fold. It's cheesy, flavorful, and packed with bacon, and it's probably my favorite side dish to serve with a juicy medium-rare steak. Try it next time you grill beef or chicken. You will instantly get it!

8 slices bacon, cut into small pieces

1 medium yellow onion, finely diced

1 red bell pepper, finely diced

One 30-ounce can hominy, drained and rinsed

¾ cup half-and-half

Hot sauce

Kosher salt and ground black pepper

½ cup grated cheddar cheese

½ cup grated Monterey Jack cheese

3 tablespoons butter, melted

½ cup panko breadcrumbs

1. Preheat the oven to 375°F.

2. In a large skillet over medium-high heat, cook the bacon until just crisp.

4. To the bacon fat in the pan, add the onion and bell pepper . . .

6. Turn the heat to low and add the hominy . . .

3. Remove the bacon to a paper towel–lined plate.

5. And cook until soft and golden, 5 to 6 minutes.

7. The half-and-half . . .

8. Some hot sauce, and a pinch of salt and pepper.

12. Pour into a small baking dish . . .

14. And scatter the breadcrumbs over the top of the casserole. Bake for 20 minutes . . .

9. Stir to mix . . .

13. Then toss the panko in the melted butter . . .

15. Until the crumbs are golden and the casserole is bubbling. Let the hominy sit for 5 minutes before serving.

10. Then add both cheeses and the bacon . . .

11. And stir to combine.

Ol' Red.
Love this boy.

Summer Succotash

20 MINUTES **MAKES 6 TO 8 SERVINGS**

Veggie sides are difficult, because often if they involve anything beyond a simple sauté or steam, they can quickly escalate into a cheesy casserole where the veggie itself gets lost in a whole lot of richness and distraction. Not that I mind being distracted by cheese, but sometimes I just want a pile of fresh vegetables without much of anything else. Enter this succotash, which is always a delight from a visual perspective, with a light lemony sauce that brings out the very best in whatever combination of vegetables you use. Some combination of corn and shelled beans is usually involved, and then you can throw in whatever your garden or produce drawer dictates. There's nothing this doesn't go with! (It's like a good pair of jeans that way.)

2 tablespoons olive oil

2 tablespoons butter

1 red onion, finely diced

Kernels from 1 ear of corn (or 1 cup thawed frozen corn kernels)

One 8-ounce bag shelled edamame

Kosher salt and ground black pepper

1 red bell pepper, finely diced

1 zucchini, finely diced

1 yellow squash, finely diced

4 garlic cloves, finely minced

2 jalapeños, cut into thin rounds

1 cup multicolored cherry tomatoes, halved

Juice of 1 lemon

1. Heat the olive oil and butter in a large skillet over medium-high heat. Add the onion, corn, and edamame . . .

3. Add the bell pepper, then stir and cook for 1 minute . . .

5. Stir and cook until the zucchini and squash are starting to soften, about 3 more minutes.

2. Sprinkle in a pinch of salt and pepper and cook, stirring constantly, for 2 minutes.

4. Then add the zucchini, squash, garlic, and jalapeños!

6. Add the tomatoes and stir them in.

7. Then squeeze in the lemon! Give the succotash a final stir and serve it warm.

SUCCOTASH VARIATIONS!

- Shave Parmesan over the finished dish.

- Add lots of torn basil over the top.

- Add chunks of crumbled goat cheese before serving.

- Cut 2 slices of bacon into small bits and cook it for 3 minutes to render the fat. Add it at the end; the bacon will add amazing flavor!

Fred may be Ladd's . . . but Rusty is all mine! (We have the same freckles.)

Page 267

When all you want is a
beautiful veggie side!

Page 279 →

Made with a miraculous shortcut!

INSTANT CHEESY MASH

🕙 10 MINUTES **MAKES 4 TO 6 SERVINGS**

Friends! I need you to look at the whites of my eyes for a second: Before you read the ingredient list below, please look at the large photo opposite and believe me when I tell you that these mashed potatoes are magnificent. Trust me, you will not encounter another person on earth who loves and believes in from-scratch mashed potatoes more than I do, but for those times you've gotta have a bed of mashed potatoes and you have neither the time nor patience to peel, dice, boil, mash, and mix, this recipe will get you through with flying colors. Again, I am a mashed potato snob . . . and I am in love with these. Instant mashed potatoes are not the massive compromise they used to be, especially when you load them with cheese and seasonings. Go for it—at least once! (Because I know that will lead to twice, thrice, and so forth.)

2 cups instant mashed potatoes (potato flakes)

Kosher salt and ground black pepper

2 teaspoons garlic powder

2 teaspoons onion powder

1½ cups grated cheddar cheese

2 tablespoons butter

1 tablespoon minced fresh chives

1. Bring 4 cups water to a boil, then turn off the heat. Add the instant potatoes . . .

3. Pile in the cheddar . . .

VARIATIONS

- Add 5 to 7 cloves Garlic Confit (page 3) with the cheeses.
- Add 4 ounces goat cheese with the cheddar.
- Stir in Caramelized Onions (page 12) and bacon bits for a loaded cheesy mash!

2. Along with a pinch of salt and pepper, the garlic powder, and onion powder.

4. And stir for about a minute, until everything is melted. Let the potatoes sit for 1 minute more, then taste, adjust the seasonings, and stir one last time. Serve immediately with the butter and chives on top.

LEMON PEPPER CORN ON THE COB

🕐 10 MINUTES **MAKES 6 TO 8 SERVINGS**

It's pretty hard to turn frozen corn on the cob into anything exciting, but this super-quick recipe does exactly that. Serve these with ribs, burgers, steaks, or chicken. Lemony and wonderful!

8 frozen corn on the cob sections

½ cup (1 stick) butter, at room temperature

3 garlic cloves, pressed or grated

2 teaspoons lemon pepper seasoning

Pinch of red pepper flakes

Grated zest of 1 lemon

¼ cup grated Parmesan cheese, for garnish

1. Bring a large pot of water to a boil and add the frozen mini ears of corn. Boil the corn until tender, about 5 minutes.

3. Smush it all together until well combined.

5. Sprinkle on the Parmesan! By the time you sit down to the table, the butter will be melted and all the yummy spices will be coating the kernels.

Note: The butter mixture can be halved if you aren't a complete butter lunatic like I am!

2. Meanwhile, in a medium bowl, combine the butter, garlic, lemon pepper, pepper flakes, and lemon zest.

4. Remove the corn from the boiling water and immediately spread a tablespoon of the butter mixture on each piece. (Psst. This butter also tastes delicious spread on warm rolls!)

Totally redeems frozen corn!

PIMENTO CHEESE GRITS

⏱ 35 MINUTES **MAKES 8 TO 10 SERVINGS**

As we say at The Mercantile, grits are really just an excuse to eat a bowl of butter and cheese—or, in the case of this variation, a bowl of cream cheese and cheese! What could possibly be wrong with that? If you've spent your life grits-free so far, the time has come to change your ways! Grits are everything, and you can eat them with fried eggs for breakfast, burgers for lunch, or lamb chops for dinner. These have a pimento cheese vibe with irresistible bits of bacon, and I wish I could be present to witness your first bite.

8 slices bacon, cut into small pieces

4 garlic cloves, minced

3 green onions, sliced, dark greens kept separate

6 cups low-sodium chicken broth

Kosher salt and ground black pepper

1½ cups quick grits

2 tablespoons adobo sauce from a can of chipotle peppers

Two 4-ounce jars sliced pimentos, drained

8 ounces cream cheese, at room temperature

2 cups grated sharp cheddar cheese

1 cup grated Monterey Jack cheese

1 heaping tablespoon Dijon mustard

1. Cook the bacon in a deep skillet over medium-high heat until just crisp.

3. Add the garlic and the whites and light-green parts of the green onion, then stir and cook for 2 minutes to release the flavors.

5. Then stir and heat until the mixture is just about to boil.

2. Drain the bacon on paper towels and pour off most of the fat left in the pan.

4. Add the broth and a pinch of salt and pepper . . .

6. Slowly add the grits, stirring constantly . . .

Page 267!

I like a little grits with my cheese!

7. And cook until the grits are tender and the excess liquid has been absorbed, 5 to 7 minutes. Reduce the heat to low.

8. Add the adobo sauce and pimentos and stir . . .

9. Then add the cream cheese. Let it sit in the grits for 1 minute . . .

10. And stir until the grits are creamy.

11. Add the cheddar cheese, Monterey Jack cheese, and mustard . . .

12. And stir . . .

13. Then add the bacon, reserving a few pieces for garnish. Serve with a sprinkle of bacon and the dark greens of the sliced green onion.

That's a side-eye if I ever saw one!

Faster FUNERAL POTATOES

🕐 30 MINUTES **MAKES 8 TO 10 SERVINGS**

First, I'm not sure the words "faster" and "funeral" should ever exist side by side as they do in the title of this dish, but I wasn't sure how else to convey that this is a slightly more expeditious path to the classic potato potluck casserole. Whereas the original funeral potatoes recipe calls for dumping all the ingredients (including frozen hash browns) into a casserole dish and baking, this hastens things along by pre-cooking things a bit in a skillet before they ever go in the oven. It's perfect with chicken, steak, or pork chops, and I dare ya not to tell your guests that the potatoes came out of a bag. Once the casserole comes out of the oven, it's almost impossible to tell.

1 small yellow onion

2 tablespoons butter

One 30-ounce bag shredded hash browns

Two 4-ounce jars pimentos, drained

Two 10.5-ounce cans condensed cream of chicken soup

1 cup sour cream

½ cup grated cheddar cheese

½ cup grated Monterey Jack cheese

Ground black pepper

2 cups cornflakes

1. Preheat the oven to 375°F.

2. Peel and grate the onion using the largest holes on a box grater.

4. Then add the grated onion.

6. Add the pimentos and the soup . . .

3. Heat the butter in a 10-inch cast-iron skillet over medium-high heat. Dump in the hash browns . . .

5. Cook the potatoes for about 3 minutes, stirring gently. This step will mostly serve to thaw the potatoes.

7. And give it a stir. Add the sour cream and three-quarters of the cheeses.

8. Season with a generous pinch of black pepper and stir.

9. Spread the mixture into an even layer and sprinkle on the cornflakes . . .

10. And the remaining cheese. Bake until the topping is melted and golden and the potatoes are bubbly, 20 to 23 minutes. Serve hot!

Along for the ride!

A quicker version
of the classic!

Delightful Desserts

I didn't do an exact count, but if my estimation is correct, there are more recipes in this chapter than any other chapter in the book. And why is that, one might wonder? Oh, I remember: Sugar is why! And maybe a little butter. And cream. And chocolate. And caramel. And . . . okay, I'll stop now. Just know that at one time during the writing process, this chapter was even longer, and the recipes that remained once I made the necessary cuts are truly, truly beyond!

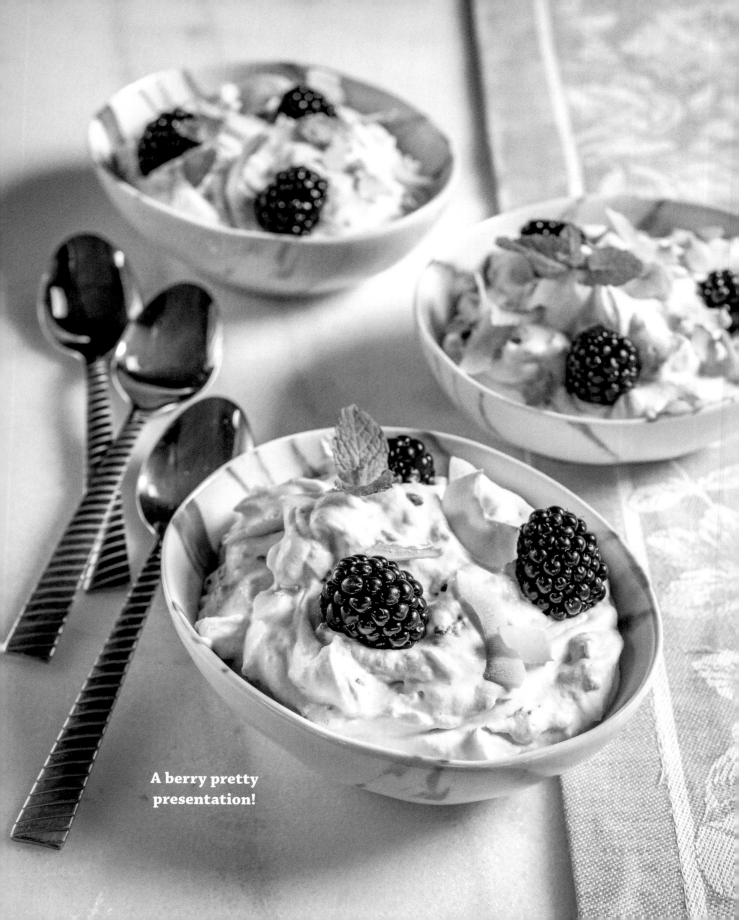

A berry pretty
presentation!

BLACKBERRY LIME WHIP

⏱ 15 MINUTES **MAKES 4 TO 8 SERVINGS**

This delectable berries-and-cream dessert is reminiscent of raspberry fool, without the crumbled ladyfingers stirred throughout . . . and *with* (and thank goodness for this "with"!) the unmistakable addition of coconut rum. It reminds me of a tropical blackberry piña colada, or at least what I imagine a tropical blackberry piña colada tastes like in my dreams of escaping to sunny destinations. I love this dessert because you can serve little or large portions depending on how much dessert your guests are looking to eat. It's the perfect fruity, creamy bite or two!

¼ cup sugar

4 cups fresh blackberries, plus more for garnish

5 tablespoons coconut rum

Grated zest and juice of 1 lime

2 cups (1 pint) heavy cream

¼ cup powdered sugar

½ cup toasted coconut chips

4 to 8 small mint sprigs, for garnish

1. Combine the sugar, blackberries, and rum in a large bowl.

2. Add the lime zest and juice . . .

3. And use a fork to mash about half the berries. If they aren't very ripe, don't worry! The rum and the sugar will soften 'em up. Set the berries aside to macerate for 10 minutes, mashing them again once or twice.

4. In a large bowl, combine the cream and powdered sugar . . .

5. And whip until stiff peaks form.

6. Give the berries one more mash. Look at all that juice!

7. Add half of the blackberry mixture to the cream mixture . . .

9. Add the rest of the berries . . .

11. Dish the mixture into small bowls and arrange fresh blackberries on top.

8. And fold it just three times. You don't want to stir or totally mix the berries and cream!

10. And fold it three more times. Make yourself stop here! You'll think it can handle one or two more stirs, but don't do it! You want to see all the white and purple swirls.

12. Sprinkle on toasted coconut and garnish with mint!

It's Bring Your Sons to Work Day!

APPLE FRITTERS

⏱ 25 MINUTES **MAKES 12 TO 14 FRITTERS**

If I were compiling a list of treats that I'm 100 percent powerless to resist, these little fried apple doughnuts dipped in caramel sauce would vie for the top spot. There's something about the warm, fried fritter with the crispy, craggy edges and the teeny bits of apple that touch something deep within my dessert-loving (and doughnut-loving) soul. For this reason, I allow myself to make these fritters only on days that end in the letter "y." (I'm disciplined like that.)

Vegetable oil, for deep-frying
1 large Granny Smith apple
¾ cup packaged pancake mix
¼ cup sugar
1 teaspoon ground cinnamon
1 large egg, beaten
3 tablespoons whole milk
1 teaspoon vanilla extract
Powdered sugar, for dusting
Caramel sauce, for serving

3. In a large bowl, combine the pancake mix, sugar, and cinnamon. Stir to mix.

6. And stir until everything comes together. The consistency should be like a thick pancake batter.

1. Heat 3 inches of oil in a medium pot over medium heat until the temperature reaches 375°F. Set a wire rack on a sheet pan.

4. Add the egg and milk . . .

7. Add the bits of apple . . .

2. While the oil is heating, dice the apple very small. The apple will need to soften in the small amount of time it fries, so teeny bits work great!

5. And the vanilla . . .

8. And fold them in until they're evenly distributed.

9. Use a 2-tablespoon scoop to remove portions of the batter . . .

10. And carefully drop them into the oil, with the scoop very close to the surface to avoid splattering. Start by frying 8 or 9 fritters, or fewer if it's easier for you!

11. Use a spider strainer or slotted spoon to begin moving the fritters around as they fry, to keep them from sticking together. They should start to brown on one side after 1 minute; watch and start turning them before they get too brown.

12. The fritters should fry for about 2 minutes per side, until deep golden and crisp on the surface.

13. Remove the fritters to the rack. Let them sit for 3 minutes after they come out of the oil, just to ensure the center batter is no longer raw.

14. Dust with powdered sugar and serve with caramel sauce while they're nice and warm! Repeat by frying the rest of the batter and serving as they're finished.

~~~~~~~~~~~~~~~~~~~~~~~~~~~~

VARIATIONS

- Try multigrain pancake mix for a slightly different fritter texture.

- Omit the apples and call them doughnut holes! Serve with chocolate syrup.

Hurry up and wait!

Pancake mix makes these a super-fast treat!

The dough comes
together in a saucepan!

SALTED WHITE CHOCOLATE SAUCEPAN COOKIES

 25 MINUTES **MAKES 12 COOKIES**

I'm not only an impatient home cook, I'm also an impatient home baker!! As such, I'm always looking for little ways to shave time off the recipes I love to eat. Now, one could say I'm old, tired, and lazy. Or . . . one could say I'm innovative and brilliant! I choose to believe the latter, but let's just say I'm probably somewhere more in the middle. Either way, saucepan cookies have transformed my cookie-making life, and here's why: You melt the butter rather than beat it, which saves time in itself, but when you also factor in how long butter can take to soften before you can even start the process, let's just say that we're looking at saving a bunch of time! This pleasantly sweet and slightly salty sugar cookie is a great foray into the world of saucepan cookies. Try them soon!

½ cup (1 stick) salted butter

¼ cup granulated sugar

⅓ cup powdered sugar

1 tablespoon packed brown sugar

1 large egg

1 tablespoon clear vanilla extract (or regular vanilla)

1 cup self-rising flour

½ teaspoon kosher salt

⅓ cup white chocolate chips

¼ cup rainbow sprinkles, plus more for . . . sprinkling!

¼ teaspoon flaky sea salt

1. Preheat the oven to 350°F. Line two sheet pans with parchment paper.

2. In a large saucepan, melt the butter over medium heat.

3. Remove the pan from the heat and add the granulated sugar, powdered sugar, and brown sugar.

4. Whisk until it's all combined.

5. Crack in the egg and whisk it in immediately . . .

6. Then add the vanilla . . .

7. Along with the flour and the kosher salt.

8. Stir everything together with a rubber spatula until smooth, then add the white chocolate chips and sprinkles . . .

11. Add a few extra sprinkles . . .

12. And bake the cookies until golden, 10 to 12 minutes. As soon as they come out of the oven, sprinkle a teeny bit of sea salt on each cookie.

9. And fold until everything is mixed. The white chocolate chips will be mostly melted, and that's exactly what you want!

10. Drop 6 scoops onto each sheet pan, leaving room for the cookies to spread.

Not on the porch!!!

SAUCEPAN BROWN BUTTER CHOCOLATE CHUNK COOKIES

⏱ 15 MINUTES **MAKES 12 COOKIES**

Warm chocolate chip cookies are one of this earthly life's true pleasures, so an easier/faster version is just what the doctor ordered! This saucepan cookie version starts not only with melted butter, but with *browned* melted butter, which pretty much guarantees these are gonna be a hit.

A quick note about saucepan cookies: Because of the melted butter, they are by nature flatter than regular cookies. But they're still completely delicious: chewy, slightly crisp, and lovely!

½ cup (1 stick) salted butter

⅓ cup packed brown sugar

⅓ cup powdered sugar

1 large egg

1 tablespoon vanilla extract

1 cup all-purpose flour

½ teaspoon baking soda

¼ teaspoon kosher salt

3 ounces bittersweet chocolate or semisweet chocolate, chopped into small chunks

¼ teaspoon flaky sea salt

1. Preheat the oven to 350°F. Line two sheet pans with parchment paper.

2. Melt the butter in a large saucepan over medium heat. Cook the butter, stirring occasionally, until it starts to turn brown, about 5 minutes. Turn off the heat when the color resembles caramel and the butter solids are medium golden brown. Note that the butter solids can burn quickly once they get to this stage, so have the rest of your ingredients ready so you can proceed with step 3 as soon as you turn off the heat.

3. Add the brown sugar and powdered sugar . . .

4. And whisk until smooth.

5. Add the egg and vanilla . . .

6. And whisk until smooth.

7. Add the flour, baking soda, and kosher salt . . .

8. And use a rubber spatula to mix everything until it just comes together.

9. Add three-quarters of the chocolate chunks and fold them in . . .

10. Then immediately drop 6 scoops of the dough onto each sheet pan, leaving room for the cookies to spread.

11. Arrange 3 or 4 of the remaining chocolate chunks on top of each cookie . . .

12. And bake the cookies until the edges are crisp but the cookies are still gooey, 10 to 12 minutes. Sprinkle a teeny bit of sea salt on top of each cookie.

Post-work smile! (That's a good sign.)

No waiting for the
butter to soften!

The cookie of my adolescence!

PEANUT BUTTER CUP COOKIES

🕐 25 MINUTES **MAKES 24 COOKIES**

There is nary a cookie on earth that catapults me back to my teenage years like these little peanut butter cup cookies baked in a mini muffin pan. Back then we used store-bought rolls of peanut butter cookie dough, but the manufacturer of that company is out to get me and doesn't care about my happiness, so I haven't been able to consistently locate it for years and years! Yes, one can make from-scratch peanut butter cookie dough, but that takes a lot of softening and measuring and time, and life is way too short for such things! So I found a workaround: This ready-in-three-minutes (seriously), no-flour dough that will change your life. Give it a try—you'll be amazed!

24 mini peanut butter cups (individually wrapped)

1 cup crunchy peanut butter

¾ cup packed brown sugar

1 large egg

Flaky sea salt, for sprinkling

1. Preheat the oven to 350°F. Unwrap the peanut butter cups and set them aside. (Great job for kids if you trust them!)

2. In a large bowl, combine the peanut butter, brown sugar, and egg.

4. Add tablespoon-size pinches of dough to the wells of a 24-cup mini muffin pan. No need to roll them into balls—just rough little piles are best!

6. And immediately press a peanut butter cup into the center of each cookie so that each cup has a rim of cookie surrounding it.

3. Use a hand mixer to thoroughly beat the mixture until all the elements are totally combined. Scrape the sides of the bowl with a rubber spatula, then mix again to ensure everything is smooth.

5. Bake until the edges are golden and crisp and the cookies are puffed, about 10 minutes. Take them out of the oven . . .

7. Sprinkle the top of each cookie with a little sea salt, then let them sit for 10 to 15 minutes before removing them from the pan. Use a table knife or spoon to gently scoop them out.

CHUCKWAGON BROWNIES

 35 MINUTES (PLUS 15 MINUTES TO COOL) **MAKES 12 LARGE BROWNIES**

The batter for these brownies is mixed right in a saucepan, much like their saucepan cookie counterparts (see pages 329 and 331), which—fortunately or unfortunately, whatever your perspective—makes them incredibly easy to get in the oven. They bake up gooey and rich, with a deep flavor helped along by the addition of espresso powder. But the real star of these rich little rascals is the unapologetic layer of chocolate pieces that are baked right on top. I don't know who I think I am with this recipe, but "chocolate freak" must be in there somewhere.

1 cup (2 sticks) salted butter

1⅓ cups granulated sugar

⅓ cup powdered sugar

2 large eggs

1 tablespoon vanilla extract

One 4-ounce bittersweet chocolate bar, roughly chopped

1 cup all-purpose flour

⅓ cup unsweetened cocoa powder

1 tablespoon instant espresso powder (or instant coffee)

½ teaspoon kosher salt

Two 4-ounce semisweet chocolate bars, broken into pieces

1. Preheat the oven to 400°F. Lay a long sheet of parchment sideways in a 9 × 13-inch baking pan, allowing it to hang over the long sides by 2 to 3 inches. (This will make it easier to remove the brownies from the pan after baking.)

2. In a large saucepan, melt the butter over medium heat until just bubbling.

3. Remove the pan from the heat and add the two sugars.

4. Whisk to combine . . .

5. Then crack in the eggs and whisk them in . . .

6. And add the vanilla and bittersweet chocolate.

An absolute chocolate explosion!

7. Whisk until the chocolate is melted and the mixture is smooth . . .

8. Then add the flour, cocoa powder, espresso powder, and salt.

9. Use a rubber spatula to fold everything together until just incorporated, taking care not to beat or overmix.

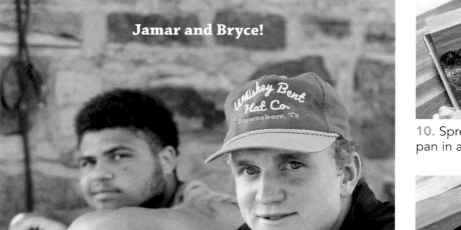

Jamar and Bryce!

10. Spread the batter into the pan in an even layer . . .

11. Then dot the top with the semisweet chocolate chunks!

12. Bake the brownies until they are set but still really gooey in the middle, taking care not to burn the surface, about 22 minutes. Let them cool for about 15 minutes, then cut into squares!

BUDINO

25 MINUTES (PLUS 1 HOUR TO CHILL) **MAKES 4 LARGE DESSERTS**

Budino is Italian for "pudding," so right off the bat you need to know that this dessert isn't fancy or fussy. This salted caramel–topped presentation was made famous in recent years by pastry chef Dahlia Narvaez, and it's a truly beautiful and impressive sweet! When I make it, I use my basic, very pared-down pudding recipe, which is the same one I make whether I'm going the vanilla route or the chocolate route. It's not pastry chef quality . . . but it's home-cook friendly! Make this once and you'll want to make it again and again!

1½ cups packed brown sugar

¼ cup cornstarch

½ teaspoon kosher salt

4 large egg yolks

3 cups whole milk

2 tablespoons salted butter

½ cup salted caramel sauce, for serving

Flaky sea salt, for serving

Canned whipped cream, for serving (optional)

1. In a large saucepan, combine the brown sugar, cornstarch, and kosher salt.

3. In a pitcher, combine the egg yolks . . .

5. And whisk until well mixed.

2. Whisk it to mix.

4. And the milk . . .

6. Add the egg mixture to the saucepan, whisking to combine.

7. Turn the heat to medium and cook, stirring gently, until the mixture fully heats and starts to bubble and thicken. It should have a thick but pourable pudding consistency. Stir in the butter until it melts.

9. When chilled, drizzle the caramel sauce all over the surface of the pudding, creating a thin but visible layer.

10. Sprinkle on a little sea salt and serve with whipped cream if you like!

FUN SERVING VARIATIONS

- *Pour the pudding mixture into shot glasses for a cute cocktail party dessert.*
- *Top the pudding with chocolate syrup or ganache instead of caramel.*

8. Divide the mixture equally among four glasses or dessert dishes, then place them in the fridge for at least 1 hour or up to 24 hours.

Del and Ladd—they've worked together for thirty years!

Excellent
for entertaining!

CHERRY PIE COOKIE BARS

 55 MINUTES (PLUS 20 MINUTES TO COOL) **MAKES 12 BARS**

It's hard to assign a category to this lovely treat, and that's what's so wonderful about it. Is it a cookie? A bar? A cobbler? A pie? I love it when desserts keep me guessing! I don't really have a definite answer, but I do know that canned cherry pie filling, in all its bright-red, happy, gelatinous glory, makes this world a better place.

Softened butter for the baking dish

1⅓ cups (2⅔ sticks) salted butter, at room temperature

1½ cups granulated sugar

Grated zest of ½ orange

2 large eggs

1 teaspoon vanilla extract

4 cups all-purpose flour

1 tablespoon baking powder

½ teaspoon kosher salt

2 tablespoons whole milk

One 30-ounce can cherry pie filling

GLAZE

1 cup powdered sugar

1 tablespoon whole milk, plus more if needed

Grated zest of 1 lemon

1. Preheat the oven to 375°F. Grease a 9 × 13-inch baking dish.

2. In a large bowl, combine the butter, granulated sugar, and orange zest.

4. Crack in the eggs . . .

6. In a separate bowl, sift together the flour, baking powder, and salt.

3. Beat with a hand mixer until well combined.

5. Then add the vanilla and beat again until well mixed.

7. Add half the dry ingredients and half the milk . . .

The cherries are so cheery!

8. And beat to combine. Repeat with the rest of the dry mixture and milk.

10. Spread the cherry pie filling all over the dough . . .

12. Until the dough on the top is golden.

9. Press two-thirds of the dough into the baking dish.

11. Then add the rest of the dough in clumps all over the top of the cherries. Bake for 35 to 37 minutes . . .

13. Make the glaze: Whisk the powdered sugar, milk, and lemon zest in a medium bowl until smooth. Add a teaspoon more of milk at a time if needed for thinning.

14. Drizzle the glaze all over the top. Let the pan sit for 20 minutes before cutting into 12 bars.

The famous Dessert Drool! I know it well, Fred.

CHOCOLATE-HAZELNUT BRAID

🕐 30 MINUTES **MAKES 6 SERVINGS**

Frozen puff pastry is a dream ingredient, because it takes 30 to 45 minutes to thaw and replaces an ingredient that would take about 4 hours to make from scratch. You wind up with a beautifully puffed, flaky pastry that no one knows came from a frozen store-bought dough . . . and to repeat: It's simply a dream. I love making puff pastry braids, as you can fill them with anything from jam to cream cheese to pie filling. But my favorite filling of late is Nutella. Oh, what a beautiful word.

One 9-inch-square sheet frozen puff pastry, thawed

All-purpose flour, for dusting

½ cup Nutella

¼ cup salted roasted peanuts, chopped

1 large egg, beaten

Pinch of flaky sea salt

ICING

½ cup powdered sugar

½ teaspoon vanilla extract

Splash of milk

1. Preheat the oven to 375°F. Line a sheet pan with parchment paper.

2. Lay out the puff pastry sheet and spread the Nutella over the center third of the sheet, leaving a ½-inch border on both ends.

4. Use a knife to make 8 even cuts across both outer sections, to create 9 strips on each side.

6. Then continue to create a simple braided look. Tuck the last strip underneath the middle section of the braid.

3. Sprinkle the chopped peanuts all over the Nutella.

5. Criss-cross the top two strips diagonally . . .

7. Transfer the braid to the sheet pan and brush it generously with the beaten egg.

8. Sprinkle the surface with a little sea salt, then bake the braid until golden and puffed, about 25 minutes.

9. Make the icing: Mix the powdered sugar, vanilla, and milk. The icing should be very thick but still able to be drizzled.

10. Drizzle on the icing, then cut into slices and serve.

Feeling beachy!

That's Nutella
in there!

No-CHURN ICE CREAM BOWLS

 20 MINUTES (PLUS 2 HOURS TO FREEZE) **MAKES 4 ICE CREAM BOWLS**

This is truly one of the most delightful desserts I've made in recent memory, because the ice cream is a cinch and the final presentation is just so fun and festive. These cute little bowls, all coated in chocolate and loaded with ice cream and cherries, make me feel young again, I tell ya. Which means I need to eat one of these every day for the rest of my life.

1 cup semisweet chocolate chips

2 teaspoons coconut oil, plus more as needed

1 cup heavy cream

1 teaspoon vanilla extract

½ cup sweetened condensed milk

4 waffle cone bowls

40 Luxardo or regular Maraschino cherries, plus more for topping

Dark chocolate syrup

Canned whipped cream, for serving

Rainbow sprinkles, for serving

1. In a double boiler (or a heatproof bowl set over a pan of simmering water), combine the chocolate chips and coconut oil. They will slowly start to melt.

2. Meanwhile, whip the cream and vanilla until stiff peaks form, about 4 minutes.

3. Add the sweetened condensed milk . . .

4. And fold the mixture until just combined. Set it in the fridge to stay cool.

5. Stir the chocolate until smooth. It should be silky and fall off the spoon. If it's too thick, add another teaspoon of coconut oil and stir.

6. Spoon a couple of tablespoons of the chocolate into one of the waffle cone bowls.

The easiest ice cream,
the cutest cups!

7. Tilt the bowl so that the chocolate coats the inside, coming as close to the top edge as you can. Spoon in another spoonful of chocolate if needed to fully coat.

8. Repeat to coat the rest of the bowls. Place the bowls on a small tray and freeze them for a few minutes, until the chocolate is hard.

9. Spoon about ¼ cup of the cream mixture into each cup . . .

10. Stick 5 cherries on the surface . . .

11. Drizzle chocolate syrup over the cherries . . .

12. Then make another layer of ⅓ cup cream mixture, 5 cherries, and a drizzle of chocolate syrup.

13. Freeze the cups uncovered for 2 hours to harden, then serve immediately or wrap individually in plastic wrap to store for up to 4 months. Add whipped cream and sprinkles before serving!

We have to go to the mountains to escape the stressful prairie!

Espresso Sundaes

⏱ 10 MINUTES **MAKES ABOUT 2½ CUPS OF SAUCE, ENOUGH FOR 6 TO 8 SUNDAES**

Coffee ice cream is my favorite kind of ice cream, and this incredibly easy hot fudge sauce will completely recharge your ice cream sundae life forever. I made it for my mom and sister once when I was filming my cooking show, and as we ate it, we all looked at one another in disbelief. Must be tasted to be believed!

One 4-ounce bar semisweet chocolate, broken into pieces

⅔ cup very hot espresso or strong coffee

Vanilla bean ice cream

Chocolate-covered espresso beans, for serving

Biscoff cookies, for serving

1. Place the chocolate in a large bowl and pour the espresso or coffee on top. (Sometimes I'll microwave the coffee for 2 to 3 minutes to ensure it's extremely hot.)

3. Until it's melted and very smooth.

5. Dot the top with a few chocolate-covered espresso beans . . .

2. Let it sit undisturbed for 5 minutes to soften the chocolate, then whisk . . .

4. Scoop ice cream into a bowl or sundae cup and drizzle on the chocolate sauce.

6. And stick a couple of cookies into the sides.

VARIATIONS

- *Serve with coffee ice cream for a super-strong coffee treat!*
- *Serve with dulce de leche ice cream if you want to be transported to Heaven.*
- *Top with M&M's or chocolate-covered caramels instead of espresso beans.*

Makes the coffee
lover in me very
happy!

Each piece is like a stack of pancakes!

MAPLE PANCAKE CAKE

⏱ 40 MINUTES · **12 SERVINGS**

Here's another one of those delightful recipes that's impossible to fit neatly into one category. Is it a coffee cake for breakfast? A rich and luscious cake for dessert? Is it even a cake, or is it just a super-thick pancake cooked in a dish instead of on a griddle? Is it heavenly? Or is it sinful?

But really, none of that matters. All that matters is that you get a slice of it in front of you as soon as possible. It's a dead ringer for a pancake . . . in cake form. (But is it a coffee cake? Or a regular cake? Uh-oh, here I go again.)

¾ cup (1½ sticks) butter, melted

2 large eggs

2 cups plus 2 tablespoons whole milk, plus more as needed

2 tablespoons vanilla extract

1½ teaspoons maple extract

2¼ cups all-purpose flour

1½ tablespoons baking powder

¼ cup granulated sugar

½ teaspoon kosher salt, plus a pinch for the glaze

½ cup maple syrup

2 cups powdered sugar

Chopped pecans, for garnish

1. Preheat the oven to 325°F. Grease the bottom and sides of a 9 × 13-inch baking dish with 2 tablespoons of the melted butter.

2. In a large pitcher, combine the eggs, 2 cups of the milk, 1 tablespoon of the vanilla, and 1 teaspoon of the maple extract.

4. Add the flour, baking powder, granulated sugar, salt, and 4 tablespoons (¼ cup) of the melted butter . . .

3. Using an immersion blender (or transfer the mixture to a regular blender), mix the ingredients until totally blended.

5. And blend into a smooth batter.

6. Pour the batter evenly into the pan and bake until it's barely starting to turn golden and is no longer jiggly in the middle, 22 to 24 minutes.

7. Meanwhile, to make the glaze, in a small pitcher or bowl, whisk the remaining 6 tablespoons melted butter, the maple syrup, remaining 1 tablespoon vanilla extract, remaining ½ teaspoon maple extract, and a pinch of salt.

8. Pour the butter mixture into a large bowl with the powdered sugar, whisking constantly.

9. Mix until smooth, then splash in the remaining 2 tablespoons milk and whisk again.

10. Check the consistency: It should be thick but pourable. Add a splash of milk as needed for thinning.

11. Pour the glaze over the cake when it's still hot from the oven.

12. Spread the glaze out evenly, then sprinkle chopped pecans over the surface. You can serve it immediately or let it sit for an hour or so. (It gets better as it sits and soaks in some of the glaze!)

Love you, Todd!

CHOCOLATE PEANUT BUTTER PIE

⏱ 25 MINUTES (PLUS 1 HOUR TO CHILL) **MAKES ONE 9-INCH PIE**

This was one of the earliest desserts I ever shared on my food blog back in the day, and it's perfectly reflective of the kind of no-frills, un-fancy, grandma-inspired recipes readers came to expect from me. To this day it's a pie that folks mention loving when I meet them in person, and the fact that I've never included it in one of my cookbooks is on the list of the top-ten oversights in my life. It's delicious and it's homey, and you will absolutely love it.

25 Oreos

4 tablespoons (½ stick) butter, melted

One 8-ounce package cream cheese, at room temperature

1 cup creamy peanut butter

1¼ cups powdered sugar

One 8-ounce container Cool Whip, thawed

1. Preheat the oven to 350°F.

2. Place the Oreos in a food processor (this is a mini one!) and pulse them into crumbs.

4. Dump the crumbs into a 9-inch pie pan and press them into the bottom and up the sides. Bake the crust for 5 minutes, then set it aside to cool completely.

6. And beat until they're mostly mixed . . .

3. Drizzle in the butter and pulse a few more times to moisten the crumbs.

5. Combine the cream cheese and peanut butter in a large bowl . . .

7. Then add the powdered sugar . . .

"Honey, you need a four-hour shower."

8. And beat until totally combined.

9. Now comes the fun part! Channel your grandmother (or great-grandmother!) and add the Cool Whip.

10. Mix until smooth and luscious.

11. Spread the mixture into the cooled crust and smooth out the top, then chill for at least 1 hour or overnight. For a firmer texture, freeze the pie for 30 minutes before slicing.

A chocolate–peanut
butter love song!

JESS

TREY

ED

MATT

SAVANNAH

KATE

The Crazy Cookbook Crew!!

Acknowledgments

To my culinary partner-in-crime, Trey Wilson, as well as Jess Palace, Seth and Allison Jordan, Kate Atkinson, Savannah Givens, and Matt Taylor—my heroic cookbook team! And to photographer Ed Anderson for making these recipes look especially mouthwatering. You guys are magic!!

To the incomparable Kris Tobiassen, who takes my pile of recipes, photos, and words and turns them into something gorgeous. Kris, you are beyond!

To Cassie Jones Morgan, my editor. I am eternally grateful you happened into my life, and can't imagine going through this crazy, wonderful cookbook journey with anyone else. You are simply the best. There's no other way to say it.

To my wonderful agent, Susanna Einstein, and the whole incredible team at William Morrow: Jill Zimmerman, Anwesha Basu, Liate Stehlik, Tavia Kowalchuk, Ben Steinberg, Rachel Meyers, Pam Barricklow, Jennifer Eck, Lucy Albanese, and Anna Brower. Thank you all so much for your support!

To Haley Carter, my friend and right-hand superwoman. Plain and simple: I couldn't do what I do without you.

To my family and friends. I feel the love every day, and it means the world to me.

To my kids—I love you! Come home soon. Dad needs help on the ranch!

To Ladd, my fellow empty nester. Are we having fun yet?!? ☺

To all of you, for your kindness, support, encouragement, and inspiration. I love and appreciate you!!

Universal Conversion Chart

OVEN TEMPERATURE EQUIVALENTS

250°F = 120°C

275°F = 135°C

300°F = 150°C

325°F = 160°C

350°F = 180°C

375°F = 190°C

400°F = 200°C

425°F = 220°C

450°F = 230°C

475°F = 240°C

500°F = 260°C

MEASUREMENT EQUIVALENTS

Measurements should always be level unless directed otherwise.

⅛ teaspoon = 0.5 mL

¼ teaspoon = 1 mL

½ teaspoon = 2 mL

1 teaspoon = 5 mL

1 tablespoon = 3 teaspoons = ½ fluid ounce = 15 mL

2 tablespoons = ⅛ cup = 1 fluid ounce = 30 mL

4 tablespoons = ¼ cup = 2 fluid ounces = 60 mL

5⅓ tablespoons = ⅓ cup = 3 fluid ounces = 80 mL

8 tablespoons = ½ cup = 4 fluid ounces = 120 mL

10⅔ tablespoons = ⅔ cup = 5 fluid ounces = 160 mL

12 tablespoons = ¾ cup = 6 fluid ounces = 180 mL

16 tablespoons = 1 cup = 8 fluid ounces = 240 mL

Index

L.B. is the real MVP around here!

The End